Philip Furneaux, William Blackstone

Letters to the Honourable Mr. Justice Blackstone

Concerning his exposition of the Act of Toleration, and some positions relative to religious liberty in his celebrated Commentaries on the laws of England

Philip Furneaux, William Blackstone

Letters to the Honourable Mr. Justice Blackstone
Concerning his exposition of the Act of Toleration, and some positions relative to religious liberty in his celebrated Commentaries on the laws of England

ISBN/EAN: 9783337195731

Printed in Europe, USA, Canada, Australia, Japan

Cover: Foto ©ninafisch / pixelio.de

More available books at **www.hansebooks.com**

LETTERS

To the Honourable

Mr. Justice BLACKSTONE,

CONCERNING

His EXPOSITION of the Act of
TOLERATION,

AND

Some POSITIONS relative to
RELIGIOUS LIBERTY,

In his Celebrated
COMMENTARIES on the Laws of England.

By PHILIP FURNEAUX, D.D.

LONDON:
Printed for T. CADELL, Successor to Mr. MILLAR,
in the Strand.

MDCCLXX.

THE PREFACE.

PErsecution is unwarrantable in any cause; yet it may most naturally be expected in favour of a bad one. I do not much wonder, therefore, that the church of Rome hath recourse to it in support of her manifold corruptions and usurpations. But that Protestants should have imitated her in this greatest of all her enormities, and have thereby imprudently given a sanction to her cruel treatment of themselves, is astonishing. Nevertheless, that it is true, the history of our own country abundantly testifies.

At the beginning of the Reformation, in the reign of Elizabeth, several who had been persecuted in the preceding reign, the Queen herself not excepted, discovered very intolerant principles, and made no scruple to persecute those who

A   differed

differed from them. Very oppressive and sanguinary laws were enacted against the puritans, and all nonconformists to the ecclesiastical establishment. In the subsequent reigns of the male line of Stuart, such laws were greatly multiplied, and the most severe and violent measures pursued, to accomplish that Utopian scheme, an ecclesiastical uniformity. At length, the great Mr. Locke pleaded, with a clearness and strength peculiar to himself, the cause of universal and impartial liberty of conscience, in his celebrated Letters on Toleration. Sensible and enlarged minds quickly felt the force of his argument. But it required time for the most perspicuous and cogent reasonings, to eradicate general prejudices, and to alter the sentiments and complexion of the publick. Even in the reign of our glorious deliverer King William, when the toleration was enacted, such were the confined views of the legislature, that it was clogged with exceptions against hereticks: upon whom, as well as infidels, 'very severe penalties were

were afterwards inflicted, in the same reign, by a particular statute. This, I am persuaded, was not at all owing to the King, who seems to have had more generous sentiments of mens religious rights; but to the blind zeal of the times, and to the high principles of some leading men in convocation and parliament.

However, the sentiments and temper of the nation have been since greatly meliorated, especially under the mild administration of the Princes of the House of Hanover; to which happy reform no one contributed more, than that admirable second to Mr. Locke, the late bishop of Winchester*, by his excellent writings in defence of religious as well as civil liberty. Insomuch that persecution having been discouraged by the civil power, and now become a stranger amongst us, the generality of people, no doubt, imagine, that this hideous monster hath no more counte-

* Dr. Hoadly.

nance in the laws of their country than in the spirit of the times. The truth is, the legal state of religious liberty in these kingdoms is very little understood. Men naturally presume, that, in this free and enlightened age, the rights of conscience, especially as they see them possessed without restraint or molestation, have the same legal security with their civil rights. It will perhaps surprize many of my readers, if they are unacquainted with the Laws of their country, or have not read the late excellent Commentaries upon them, to hear, that Deists and Arians, if they declare their sentiments, are by law incapable of holding any offices or places of trust, bringing any action, being guardians, executors, legatees, or purchasers of lands, and are to suffer three years imprisonment without bail:—that to revile, or even openly to speak in derogation of the common prayer, renders a man liable to a fine of an hundred marks for the first offence, to one of four hundred for the

the second, and for the third to a forfeiture of all his goods and chattels, and imprisonment for life:—and that the toleration-act itself is so limited, that many who are commonly thought to enjoy under it, deservedly, every security which the law can give them, are yet subject to very severe and heavy inflictions, to their utter ruin, as the law now stands:—And as for those comprehended within that act; if, according to the opinion of some lawyers, they are only exempted by it from the penalties of certain laws, and are not restored to a legal consideration and capacity; upon this idea, I say, they lie open to such inabilities and oppressions, that, were advantage taken of them, their very enemies would hardly wish their situation to be more deplorable. However, this confined exposition of the toleration-act, though still maintained, it seems, by some of the profession, hath been happily condemned by most of the Judges, and is inconsistent with those grounds, on which was founded, ed, in a particular case, a solemn judgment of the supreme court of judicature. And under this discouragement it will never again, I trust, obtain the countenance of any court of law.

However that be, there are several persecuting statutes, those which I have mentioned and some others, which, I think, were a reproach to the times when they were enacted, and are much more so to the boasted freedom and liberality of sentiment of the present age, which suffers them to continue unrepealed.

Let me only ask any friend of civil liberty, what would be his reflections, if he had no security for the possession of his rights and privileges in the laws and constitution of his country, but held them only through the moderation of his superiors, or the spirit of the times? I believe, he would be extremely uneasy, till they were fixed on a legal basis; extremely attentive to the sentiments and conduct of those who, from their abilities, or

their

PREFACE.

their rank and station, might probably obstruct or promote so desirable a settlement: and those who, in any critical juncture, would be likely to act in opposition to the cause of liberty, would certainly be the objects of his jealousy, if not of his aversion. Now let every such friend of the civil rights of his country, whatever be his own religious opinions, and however secure he may himself be in his religious profession under the protection of the law, consider the case of those who are obnoxious to such penal statutes, as, being still in force, may possibly be employed (and he can never be sure they will not be employed) as instruments of persecution and oppression. Every generous mind will make the interest of others, in such cases, his own; and will be far from palliating or excusing, much more from defending, such laws as are incompatible with equity and humanity, and which, by those who would be thought friends of religious liberty, should never be be mentioned but with difapprobation and cenfure. What part the ingenious and learned Commentator on the laws of England, to whom the following Letters are addreffed, hath taken, when he is confidering fome of thofe ftatutes to which I refer, is not for me to fay: the publick, as it is fit it fhould, will judge.

No laws which are unjuft, and inconfiftent with that religious liberty which it is right the inhabitants of thefe kingdoms fhould enjoy, (and I apprehend that which they do enjoy, it is generally thought right they fhould, becaufe they have now enjoyed it for many years unmolefted;) I fay, no laws which are indefenfible, and incompatible with the rights of confcience, fhould be fuffered to remain unrepealed. For if it be proper, that fuch rights fhould be poffeffed in the extent in which they are through the lenity of the times, it is proper there fhould be a legal fecurity for the poffeffion of them; that they may not be trampled upon through the poffible caprices

PREFACE.

prices of men in power, or some unaccountable turn in the sentiments of the publick. And though I would not be understood to insinuate, that there is at present any likelihood of such an infringement; yet the rights of human nature (and religious liberty in its full extent is one of these) should never lie at the mercy of any; but on the contrary, should have every protection and ground of security, which law, and the policy of free states, can give them.

If any one say, It is right to keep a rod *in terrorem*, though it would be injustice or inhumanity to use it: I shall be apt to suspect, that, notwithstanding his fair pretences, when a proper opportunity offers, he will not fail to use it. For I am sure, if, in the concerns of religion, human *terror* be a proper motive, human *punishment* is equally so.

N. B.

N. B. The following Letters were nearly printed off, before the Gentleman, to whom they are addreſſed, was appointed to the high ſtation which he now fills in the law. This is mentioned as an apology for a form of addreſs, which the reader will perceive is not ſuitable to his preſent character.

CONTENTS.

LETTER I. Dr. Blackstone's opinion concerning the act of toleration, that it only frees Dissenters from the penalties, not from the crime of nonconformity, stated, p. 3,—9. The reason assigned for this opinion considered, p. 9,—11. The contrary opinion, That the crime of nonconformity is abolished together with the penalties, with respect to those who are qualified as the act directs, proved, (1.) from the mode of expression in that clause of the act, which repeals the penal statutes with regard to such persons, p. 11,—14. (2.) from those clauses which protect the dissenting worship: The argument of a Noble Lord in a high department of the law upon this head, p. 14,—16. (3.) from the unanimous judgment of the commissioners delegates, and of the House of Lords, in the sheriff's case: the grounds of their judgment stated, and shown to be, that Dissenters are freed from the crime as well as penalties of nonconformity, p. 16,—22. Further consideration of the state of Dissenters, and of dissenting worship, under the toleration: The opinion of a Noble Lawyer, and of the late Speaker Onslow, p. 22,—24. Conclusion, p. 25, 26.

LETTER II. Dr. B. having disclaimed the approbation of the penal statute against Arians, charged upon him by Dr. Prieſtley, the omiſſion or alteration of ſome expreſſions in his Commentaries ſhown to be neceſſary, p. 27,—29. An enquiry into the proper authority for defining hereſy, of which Dr. B. ſpeaks: proved, that there is no ſuch authority: the right of private judgment aſſerted, p. 29,—35. Hereſy not being ſufficiently defined Dr. B. thinks a defect in the law: ſhown to be an advantage to religious liberty, conſidering the lenity of the times, p. 36, 37. Suppoſing hereſy puniſhable by human authority, an enquiry into the nature of that puniſhment: Dr. B.'s ſentiments concerning it examined and refuted: temporal penalties improperly applied to caſes of hereſy, p. 37,—43. Whether it be the right of a national church, as Dr. B. intimates, to prevent the propagation of crude and undigeſted ſentiments in religious matters, p. 43,—47.

LETTER III. Dr. B.'s account of the penal ſtatute againſt the Deiſts, and his ſentiment concerning the fitneſs of their being puniſhed by the magiſtrate, p. 48,—50. His argument for ſuch puniſhment from the tendency of their principles conſidered, p. 50,—56. His argument for puniſhing thoſe who depreciate the efficacy of Chriſtianity, taken from the nature of judicial oaths, conſidered, p. 56,—61. An enquiry, whether the reproaches and calumnies which infidels throw upon religion, be a proper ground of the magiſtrate's puniſhing them; inaſmuch as they affect the honour of God, are offenſive to good men, and tend to leſſen the influence of religion,

gion, p. 61,—65. The proper temper and conduct of Christians towards those who revile their holy religion, with further reasons against the punishment of infidels by the magistrate, p. 65, 70.

LETTER IV. The penal statute against speaking in derogation of the common prayer: Dr. B. of opinion, that the continuance of it to the present time is not too severe and intolerant, p. 71, 72. The reasons for his opinion considered: (1.) That it is indecency, by setting up private judgment in opposition to publick, p. 72,—79. (2.) Arrogance, in treating with rudeness and contempt what hath a better chance to be right than the singular notions of a particular man, p. 79,—89. (3.) Ingratitude, by denying that liberty to the members of the national church, which the retainers to every petty conventicle enjoy, p. 89,—94. Even allowing Dr. B.'s reasons, the statute still too severe and intolerant, p. 94, 95. Dr. B.'s attempt to justify this statute, as a means of securing the purity and decency of the national worship, considered, p. 95,—98. Dr. B. wrong in his approbation of this statute, as a lawyer, because it is so drawn as to include persons not guilty of that crime, which he supposes is the only one intended, p. 98,—100. Dr. B.'s encomium of the reign of Elizabeth considered, p. 100, to 102.

LETTER V. Dr. B.'s opinion, that an alteration in the church constitution or liturgy would be an infringement

fringement of the act of union, confidered, upon his own ftate of it; namely, fuppofing the Britifh parliament have a competent authority to make alterations, p. 103,—107. Obfervations concerning the defign of the act, p. 107, 108. Confideration of Dr. B.'s affertion, without any regard to the defign of the act, from the nature of folemn *pacta conventa*, p. 108,—115. Dr. B.'s pofition, that thofe who divide from the church upon matters of indifference, do it upon no reafon at all, confidered, p. 115,—120.

LETTER VI. Dr. B.'s opinion, that a teft-law, excluding Diffenters from civil offices, is effential to the idea of a church-eftablifhment, examined, p. 121,—123. The injuftice of excluding any good fubjects on a religious account, afferted, p. 123, 124. Such exclufion not to be vindicated by the plea of publick good, p. 124, 125. Not conducive to the good of the ftate: not granted to the church, as a reward for her inforcing the duties of imperfect obligation, or in lieu of her refigning to the ftate her independence, and the appointment of her officers, p. 125,—130. Not purchafed by the church by her confenting to a toleration, p. 130, 131. In what fenfe an exclufive teft is for the good of the church, confidered: whether vindicable, becaufe it is for her emolument: how far it contributes, as Dr. B. fuppofes, to her fecurity or protection, p. 131, to 145. Objection from the deftruction of the ecclefiaftical conftitution in the laft century, anfwered, p. 145, 146. A facramental teft little, or no fecurity

to

to the church in its own nature, and very improperly applied to civil purposes, p. 146,—148.

LETTER VII. A passage in Dr. B.'s chapter of Præmunire considered, and that it contains a reflection on the principles of the Dissenters as destructive of the obligations of society, proved, p. 149,—154. His comparison of their principles with those of the Roman Catholics, as " aiming at a distinct, inde-
" pendent supremacy of their own, where spiritual
" men and spiritual causes are concerned," examined and confuted, p. 154,—159. That their principles are totally inconsistent with those of the Anabaptists in Germany, and Fifth-monarchy-men in England, in the last age, shewn, p. 159,—162. Dr. Priestley not singular in his interpretation of a particular passage in the Commentaries, which Dr. B. hath promised to correct, p. 162,—165. The author's reason for writing to Dr. B. : Conclusion, p. 165, 166.

ERRATA.

P. 55. l. 6. *for* fyftems *read* fyftems.
Ibid. l. 17. *for* maitenance *read* maintenance.
P. 64. l. 4. *for* ren- *read* render.
P. 77. l. 5. note, *for* P. P. *read* P P.
Ibid. l. 10. *for* decretis obfequi *read* decretis nos obfequi.

LETTERS

TO

WILLIAM BLACKSTONE, Esq;

LETTER I.

SIR,

YOUR candor, I doubt not, will readily excuse an admirer of your excellent Commentaries on the laws of England, if, from a desire of their being rendered still more excellent than they are, he gives you an opportunity of reviewing some passages, which, to him at least,

least, appear to be exceptionable, and not so judicious and accurate as other parts of your truly admirable performance. It were to be wished, that a work, so nearly perfect, were *omnibus numeris absolutum*.

My profession, Sir, is not that of the law; and if it were, it would be with diffidence, at least with much deference, I should make remarks on the composition of so great a master. The point, however, which I have in view, not only is of great importance to myself, amongst others, who dissent from the established church; but some cases of a publick nature, which have come under my observation, have given me frequent occasion to consider it with no small attention. Nevertheless, if I had not found my own sentiments authorized and supported by their congruity to the declared opinion of persons of the most accurate and comprehensive acquaintance with the laws of England, and by those general grounds and reasons, on which

LETTER I.

which the most solemn judgments have been given, I should hardly have presumed to offer to you, and to the publick, the following observations.

I remember, when, some years ago, I read your Analysis of the laws of England, and observed, that, in the third chapter of the fourth book, under the head of Offences against the established church, you mentioned " Nonconformity to its wor-" ship — through Protestant dissenting;" and added " Penalty: suspended by the " toleration-act:" I then imagined, that your sentiments of the intent and influence of that act, and of the state and condition of the Dissenters under it, were confined and narrow. However, I flattered myself, that, when you came to consider the matter more thoroughly in your larger work, you would see reason to represent the case of the Dissenters somewhat differently, and do it, as I think, more justice.

But,

But, in the fourth volume of your Commentaries, chapter the fourth, p. 53. I am sorry to find the following passage: "The penalties (*viz.* those which are laid upon the Dissenters by abundance of statutes, in particular by 31 Eliz. c. 1. 17 Char. II. c. 2. 22 Char. II. c. 1.) are all of them suspended by the statute 1 Will. & Mar. st. 2. c. 18. commonly called the toleration-act, which exempts all Dissenters (except Papists, and such as deny the Trinity) from all penal laws relating to religion, provided they take the oaths of allegiance and supremacy, and subscribe the declaration against Popery, and repair to some congregation, registered in the bishop's court or at the sessions, the doors whereof must be always open: and dissenting teachers are also to subscribe the thirty-nine articles, except those relating to church-government and infant-baptism. Thus are all persons, who will approve themselves no Papists or oppugners of the Trinity,

LETTER I.

" Trinity, left at full liberty to act as their
" consciences shall direct them in the mat-
" ter of religious worship."

This is all you say of the toleration-act in your Commentaries; and before I make any observations upon it, I beg leave to mention a passage in your answer to Dr. Priestley; who had observed*, that he " did not know that MERE *nonconformity*
" was any crime at all in the laws of Eng-
" land—since the act of toleration:"—You say †, that you " beg leave to inform Dr.
" Priestley, since it seems he is yet to learn
" it, that nonconformity is still a crime
" by the laws of England, and hath severe
" penalties annexed to it, notwithstanding
" the act of toleration, (nay expressly re-
" served by that act) in all such as do not
" comply with the conditions thereby en-
" joined. In case the legislature had in-
" tended to abolish both the crime and the
" penalty, it would at once have repealed

* Remarks, p. 49.   † Reply, p. 11, 12.

" all the penal laws enacted against non-
" conformists. But it keeps them express-
" ly in force against all Papists, oppugners
" of the Trinity, and persons of no reli-
" gion at all ; and only *exempts from their
" rigour* such serious, sober-minded Dis-
" senters, as shall have taken the oaths,
" and subscribed the declaration at the ses-
" sions, and shall regularly repair to some
" licensed *" (registered) " place of reli-
" gious worship. But though these sta-
" tutes oblige me to consider nonconformi-
" ty as a breach of the law, yet (notwith-
" standing Dr. Priestley's strictures) I shall
" still continue to think, that *reviling the*
" *ordi-*

* *Registered* is the word in the act. A *licence*, in its common acceptation, implies a power of refusal : but in the present case there is no such power : for the clerk of the peace, or the register of the archdeacon's and bishop's court, is by the act *required* to register such place of meeting, upon its being certified. Accordingly, where this hath been refused by uninformed justices and clerks of the peace, a *mandamus*, upon application, hath been always granted, as it must be, to compel their compliance. Yet in the bishop's court of the diocese of Winchester, (I know not whether in any other) notwithstanding that the toleration-
act

LETTER I.

" *ordinances of the church* is a crime of a
" much grosser nature than the other of
" mere *nonconformity.*"

So that, in your opinion, Sir, mere nonconformity is a crime, though not so great as some others, and is so considered in the eye of the law, notwithstanding the toleration-act. The *penalties*, indeed, by that act are SUSPENDED, but the CRIME subsists still.

Indeed, in one place you express yourself as if you intended a limitation: " Non-
" conformity," you say, " is still a crime,
" and hath heavy penalties annexed to it,
" notwithstanding the act of toleration,
" (nay, expressly reserved by that act) *in*

act requires only that the place of worship be *certified*, an *humble petition* is, at least lately was, insisted upon, to the Right Reverend Father in God, *&c.* alledging a variety of particulars in support of the petition, and *humbly praying*, that he would be PLEASED to licence such a place of worship. To such an unwarrantable extent hath the idea of licencing been carried. But, I hope, this practice is or will be discontinued. If it is not, and should be legally questioned in the courts at Westminster, as perhaps it may, it will be quickly found, that it cannot be supported.

" *all*

"*all such as do not comply with the condi-*
"*tions thereby enjoined.*" And this observation, in itself, is very true. But you
seem to introduce it for the sake of a consequence, which, I think, will by no
means follow from it; for in the next
words you observe, " In case the legislature
" had intended to abolish both the crime
" and the penalty, it would at once have
" repealed all the penal laws enacted a-
" gainst nonconformists." Your argument
I take to be this: Because the legislature
hath not at once repealed all the penal laws
against nonconformists, that is, as you go
on to observe, " against all Papists, op-
" pugners of the Trinity, and persons of
" no religion at all;" therefore (a strange
non-sequitur surely!) the legislature did
not intend to abolish the crime, as well as
the penalty, in those who are NO Papists,
or oppugners of the Trinity, or persons of
no religion at all, but mere nonconformists
to the established rites and modes of worship. These serious sober-minded Dissenters

ters are *only exempted from the* RIGOUR *of the penal laws.* They are still *criminals* it seems, only the *penalties* due to their crime are *suspended*; and their nonconformity is still a breach of the law.

Upon this principle, the term, suspension of penalty, used in your Analysis and Commentaries with respect to the effect of the toleration-act, may be easily accounted for, and appears consistent.

It is true, in your Commentaries you immediately add, " which" (namely, the toleration-act) " exempts all Dissenters " (except Papists, and such as deny the " Trinity) from all penal laws relating to " religion, provided they take the oaths," &c. But this seems to mean nothing more than the suspension before spoken of, and to be only exegetical of that term; to be an "exemption" (as you express it in your reply to Dr. Priestley *) " from the ri- " gour" or penalties " of those laws,"

* p. 11, 12.

but

but not from the crime on which the penalties were grounded. This, I apprehend, to be your real meaning: I should be glad to find myself mistaken. I think, the truth is, that nonconformists (namely, to the peculiar rites, discipline, and government of the church, as this word always signifies) are freed from all the effects of the penal laws, as to crime as well as penalty; but these statutes remain in force, both as to crime and penalty, with respect to those who are *more* than mere nonconformists; who are Arians, or Papists, or persons of no religion at all: and that, not on account of their nonconformity, but of their supposed heresy, or enmity to the government, or infidelity and irreligion: which is very plain; for, if they purge themselves of these, and shew, in the way prescribed by the toleration-act, that they are no Arians, Popish recusants, or infidels and persons of no religion, they are immediately, notwithstanding their non-

nonconformity, unaffected by these statutes.

The question then is, Whether nonconformity be a *crime* in those who *have complied with the conditions* of the toleration-act? or, What is the state of Dissenters *under that act?* Are they in the eye of the law criminals, though the penalties are suspended? or, Are they restored to a legal capacity, and to a freedom from all crime as well as penalty, in virtue of the toleration-act?

Now, in my opinion, to represent nonconformity as a crime, the penalties of which are merely suspended, is a defective and erroneous account of the state of the Dissenters under the toleration-act. And to show this,

The FIRST observation I would make is: That suspension of penalty is not the language of the toleration-act. The act uses a comprehensive and forcible expression, which

which excludes the *crime* as well as the *penalty*; it leaves thefe penal ftatutes *no operation at all*, with refpect to the Diffenters, who are under the toleration-act; it *repeals* and *annihilates* thofe ftatutes with regard to fuch Diffenters. The words of the toleration-act are, that thofe ftatutes fhall not be conftrued to EXTEND to fuch perfons. And if they are not to be conftrued to *extend* to them, nothing can be plainer, than that they are not to be conftrued to *affect them at all*, either as to crime or penalty. Now, if the ftatute-law doth not make this a crime, it is certain, it is no crime at all by the *common law*; becaufe the conftitution of the church, and its peculiar doctrine, worfhip, difcipline, and government, are founded wholly upon the ftatute-law, and not at all upon the common law *.

Inftead,

---

* " If it is a crime not to take the facrament at church," faid a Noble Lord in a high department of the law, (and
by

LETTER I.

Instead, therefore, of saying in the Commentaries, that the *penalties* are all of them *suspended by the toleration-act*, which exempts all Dissenters, except Papists, and such as deny the Trinity, from all penal laws, &c. should it not have been said, that all penal laws for nonconformity are

_{by parity of reason, if it had been to the particular purpose of his argument at that time, he might have said, If it be a crime not to go to church, or join in any of its publick offices)} "it must be a crime by some law; which must be
"either common or statute law; the canon law inforcing
"it depending wholly upon the statute-law. Now the sta-
"tute-law is repealed, as to persons capable of pleading,
"that they are so and so qualified; and, therefore, the
"canon law is repealed with regard to those persons. If
"it is a crime by common law, it must be so either by prin-
"ciple or usage. I never heard of any usage or custom,
"that should make it *a crime not to conform to the religion of*
"*a country not established by positive statute.* As for prin-
"ciple, it must be allowed, that the principles of natural
"and revealed religion and morality are the principles of
"common law: so that any persons opposing these prin-
"ciples are actionable at common law. But neither the
"principles of natural religion, and much less those of
"revealed religion and morality, will admit of a person's
"being persecuted for opinions differing from others with
"respect to particular modes of worship. It is against
"reason, and contrary to the fitness of things."

repealed,

repealed, with regard to those Dissenters, who are qualified as the act directs? And would it not have been proper to mention, that the dissenters are freed from prosecution in the ecclesiastical courts? and that there is nothing, therefore, in the law of England, which can make mere nonconformity a crime, any more than liable to penalty?

A SECOND observation I would make is: That both the crime and penalty of mere Protestant nonconformity to the established rites and modes of worship is abolished by the act of toleration, is evident from the protecting clauses of that act: which, in the words of a great lawyer, have rendered the Dissenters way of worship, " not " only innocent, but lawful; have put it, " not merely under the connivance, but " under the protection of the law, have " *established it*. For nothing can be plain- " er, than that the law protects nothing in " that very respect, in which it is, at the " same

"same time, in the eye of the law a crime.
"Dissenters, by the act of toleration, there-
"fore, are restored to a legal consideration
"and capacity." And this is a view of their condition under the toleration-act of great importance. For many consequences will from hence follow, which are not mentioned in the act, and which would not follow, if the act amounted to nothing more than a suspension of penalty. For instance, previous to this act, a legacy, left to dissenting ministers and dissenting congregations, was not esteemed a valid one, because the law knew no such persons, and no such assemblies; and it was left to what the law called superstitious purposes. But will it be said in any court in England, that such a legacy is not a valid one now? and yet there being nothing said of this in the toleration-act, it can only follow, consequentially, from the Dissenters being restored by that act to a legal consideration and capacity, and being no longer criminal in the eye of the law,

as they were before that act was enacted.

The THIRD obfervation which I would make is: That the unanimous judgment of the commiffioners delegates *, and of the Houfe of Lords † affirming that judgment, in the great caufe between the city of London and the Diffenters, concerning the fine inflicted by a by-law of the city on thofe who refufed the office of fheriff, was grounded entirely on this opinion, " That " the toleration-act removed the crime as " well as the penalty of mere nonconfor- " mity."

The cafe was this: By the corporation-act no perfon can be placed, chofen, or elected into any office of or belonging to the government of any corporation, who

---

* Lord Chief Baron Parker, Mr. Juftice Fofter, Mr. Juftice Bathurft, and Mr. Juftice Wilmot, now Lord Chief Juftice of the Common Pleas. They delivered their opinions *feriatim*, on the 5th of July 1762. after hearing counfel feveral days. Lord Chief Juftice Willes, who was firft in the commiffion, died before the hearing.

† On the 7th of February 1767.

hath not taken the facrament in the church of England within a year preceding the time of fuch election. The defendant * pleaded, That not having rece*i*ved the facrament at church within a year preceding, he was both uneligible and difabled from ferving; and that, being a Diffenter within the defcription of the toleration-act, and thereby freed from all obligation to take the facrament at church, his omitting it was no way criminal; and that, therefore, the difability he had incurred was a lawful plea in bar of this action, to excufe him from the fine impofed upon thofe who refufed the office of fheriff. The city having brought the caufe before the Houfe of Lords by appeal from the commiffioners delegates, who had given judgment for the defendant; the Houfe ordered this queftion to be propofed for the opinion of the Judges, How far the defendant might, in the prefent cafe, be allowed to plead his

' Allen Evans, Efq;

disability in bar of the action brought against him?

It was allowed on all hands, that if his nonconformity, and his consequent disability, was criminal, he could not plead it.

And for this reason one of the Judges * was of opinion, (contrary to the rest of his brethren), that the defendant's disability, in the present case, could not be pleaded; because, as he said, the toleration-act amounted to *nothing more than an exemption of Protestant Dissenters from the penalties of certain laws therein particularly mentioned*; and the corporation-act not being mentioned therein, the toleration-act could have no influence upon it; and therefore his disability, incurred by his nonconformity in consequence of the corporation-act, was, in his opinion, a culpable one, and rendered him liable to any penalties, to which any others are liable for refusing to serve the office of sheriff; inasmuch as no

---

* Mr. Baron Perrott.

man can difable himfelf: but if he refufed to take the facrament according to the rites of the church of England, he difabled himfelf; and the fine impofed was a punifhment upon him for the crime of his nonconformity, from which he could plead no legal exemption.

But all the other Judges * were of a contrary opinion, That the corporation-act exprefsly rendered the Diffenters uneligible and incapable of ferving; its defign being to keep them out, as perfons at that time fuppofed to be difaffected to the government: and though the difability arifing from hence could not *then* have been pleaded againft fuch an action as is now brought againft the defendant, nonconformity being *then* in the eye of the law a crime, and no man being allowed to excufe one crime by another; yet the cafe is different

---

* Mr. Juftice Hewitt, now Lord Lifford, and Chancellor of Ireland; Mr. Juftice Afton, Mr. Juftice Gould, Mr. Baron Adams, Mr. Baron Smythe, Mr. Juftice Clive.

since the toleration-act was enacted, *that act* amounting to *much more* than a mere exemption from the penalties of certain laws, and having an influence upon the corporation-act consequentially, though the corporation-act is not mentioned therein; by freeing the Dissenters from all obligation to take the sacrament at church, abolishing the crime as well as penalties of nonconformity, and allowing and protecting the dissenting worship. The defendant's disability, therefore, they said, was a lawful one, a legal and reasonable, not a criminal excuse; it was not in the sense of the law disabling himself; the meaning of that maxim, " That a man shall not dis-" able himself," being only this, that no man shall disable himself by his own wilful fault or crime; and nonconformity being no longer a crime since the toleration-act was enacted, he is disabled by judgment of parliament, namely, by the corporation-act, without the concurrence or intervention of any crime of his own; and there-

therefore he may plead this disability in bar of the present action.

So that the arguments of the Judges turned upon this single point, That the toleration-act removed the *crime* as well as the *penalties* of nonconformity; and in this they all, except one, agreed. The whole was summed up, and the reasoning on the opposite side examined and confuted, with his usual perspicuity and force of argument, by Lord Mansfield *; and upon this ground the House of Lords affirmed, *nemine contradicente*, the judgment of the commissioners delegates.

In stating, therefore, the case of the Dissenters under the toleration-act, should not some notice have been taken of the protecting clauses of that act, and of their

* I have in my possession a particular account of the reasoning of the Noble Lord upon this point, in his speech previous to his motion for the affirmance of the judgment: an account which, by many very competent judges who were present, and some of them members of the supreme court by which the cause was determined, hath been thought to be no inaccurate one; a copy of which (though not exact) was published, entirely without my knowledge, in the Whitehall Evening Post of January 9.

influence and operation upon the legal condition and capacity of the Diffenters? Surely the fufpenfion of penalties is not all that this act amounts to.

Whether the toleration-act is extenfive enough as to thofe who *fhould be* its objects, is one queftion; what is its meaning and intent, with refpect to thofe who *are* its objects, is another. Mere nonconformifts with refpect to the worfhip, difcipline, and government of the church, are certainly its objects: and I think it ought not to have been limited, as it is, in regard to the doctrinal articles of religion. But ftill, with refpect to thofe perfons whom it does comprehend, that is, the mere nonconformifts to the conftitution and rites of the church, it puts them on a very liberal footing, not on that of *connivance* only, but of *protection* alfo. And the more the idea of *legal protection* is examined, the more will it appear to juftify the ftrong expreffion, which the Noble Lord

LETTER I.

Lord before mentioned used concerning the dissenting worship, that it is ESTABLISHED. If the justices of the peace at the quarter-sessions, or the register of the bishop's court should refuse to register a dissenting place of worship, a *mandamus* always is and must be granted, upon application, in Westminster-hall, to compel them to the discharge of their duty. And is it not absurd to suppose, that a *mandamus* must issue in a case, which the law regards as criminal? Is not the law to be considered as giving its *whole sanction*, and exerting its *whole energy*, in respect to whatever justifies and requires a *mandamus*? and does not this amount, strictly speaking, to the idea of the word *established*?

When the late incomparable Speaker of the House of Commons, Mr. Onslow, was informed of the expression, which the learned and Noble Lord used on this occasion, he observed, in a conversation with which he honoured me, that this was the lan-

language he himself had always held; that, as far as the authority of the law could go in point of *protection*, the Dissenters were as *truly established* as the church of England *; and that an established church, as distinguished from their places of worship, was, properly speaking, only an *endowed church*; a church, which the law not only protected, but endowed with temporalities for its peculiar support and encouragement †.

If

---

* The penalties inflicted by the act of toleration on those who disturb any dissenting congregation for divine worship, or misuse the preacher, are precisely the same as on those who disturb the congregation, or misuse the preacher, in any cathedral, parish-church, or chapel; and dissenting ministers, as well as the clergy of the church of England, are excused from all burdensome offices.

† I suppose it is upon this idea, that, since the toleration, it hath been the invariable practice of our Sovereigns, in their speeches to their parliaments upon their accession, after declaring their affection to the church of England, and resolution to support it, to add, That they will maintain the toleration inviolable. When this was done at the commencement of the present reign, the Lords, in their address of thanks, paid a just and expressive compliment to

the

If it should so happen, after all, that I should have mistaken your meaning, and that your idea of the condition of the Dissenters under the toleration-act is the same with mine, that they are freed from the *crime* as well as penalties of their nonconformity; I apprehend, some alteration will still be necessary in your representation of the purport of the toleration-act: which representation, as it now stands, leads your reader naturally, and almost necessarily, to conclude, that your apprehension of the design of that act is not so enlarged as, in my humble opinion, it ought to be. And

the toleration, by stiling it, THAT SUREST CEMENT OF THE PROTESTANT INTEREST IN THESE KINGDOMS. And this expression, in answer to that part of the royal speech, which contained a promise of preserving and *strengthening* the constitution in *church* and state, was the more apposite, as it conveyed this certain truth, That the union of Protestants among themselves in mutual affection and esteem, however they may differ in formularies of doctrine or rites of worship, is the best support of their common interest; and that the church of England, in particular, can never be more *strengthened*, or placed on a firmer foundation, than by encouraging the generous principles of *toleration*, and an impartial regard to the right of *private judgment*.

if, upon further reflection, you are convinced of this; I am very sure, from the specimens you have already given of your candor in similar cases, you will take care to guard against any misapprehension of your judgment in future editions of your incomparable book. That openness to conviction, and that consequent disposition to correct mistakes, which you have discovered, does you more honour, in a moral view, than all your intellectual abilities, great as they are; inasmuch as integrity and ingenuity of heart deserve, and will receive from those whose good opinion is worth regarding, much more applause than the acutest discernment, or the profoundest and most accurate judgment. I am,

SIR,

With great esteem,

Your obedient humble servant,

P. F.

LETTER II.

SIR,

YOU have a difpofition, I am perfuaded, too ingenuous and liberal, to be offended at a candid, though free difcuffion of your fentiments: I fhall make no apology, therefore, for laying before you my remarks on fome other paffages, as I have already done on one particular point, in your juftly-admired Commentaries on the laws of England.

When Dr. Prieftley obferved, in his Remarks, p. 48. that you quoted with approbation * the ftatute of William the Third againft " perfons educated in the

* Comment. vol. iv. p. 50.

" Chriftian

"Christian religion, or professing the same, who shall, by writing, printing, teaching, or advised speaking, deny any one of the persons in the Holy Trinity to be God, or maintain that there are more gods than one:" by which statute they are made liable to the pains and penalties inflicted by the same statute on apostacy; that is, "for the first offence, they are rendered incapable of holding any office or place of trust; and for the second, are rendered incapable of bringing any action, being guardian, executor, legatee, or purchaser of lands; and are to suffer three years imprisonment without bail*:" I say, when Dr. Priestley remarked, that you cited this severe statute with approbation, you disclaimed the imputation in

---

* The Emperor Marcian, in an edict against the Eutychians and Apollinarists, rendered them incapable of disposing of their estates, of making a will, or of inheriting any thing by the will of others, or by deed of gift. *Concil. tom. 2. p.* 678. *edit. Hard.* Some of the clauses in the act of parliament seem to have been copied from this worthy original.

your

LETTER II.

your Reply*; and alledged, that you " barely recited the ſtatute, without either " approving or diſapproving it." It will ſurely, then, be proper to omit theſe words in your Commentaries †, which you will find a little before your citation of this ſtatute, " Every thing is now as it ſhould be, " unleſs perhaps that hereſy ought to be " more ſtrictly defined," &c. This, your readers will be apt to think, amounts to an approbation of all that follows; and particularly of the act here referred to, which is preſently after quoted as now in force; and therefore, as one of the things which, you ſay, " are as they ſhould be."

Truly, Sir, it is much to be deſired, that you would review this whole paragraph with attention. The only objection which you make to the intolerant and perſecuting laws now in force againſt hereſy is, that " hereſy is not defined in them with ſuffi-

---

* Reply, p. 6. † Comment. p. 49.

" cient

"cient precision;" and, you think, "no profecution should be permitted, even in the ecclesiastical courts, till the tenets in question are, by proper authority, previously declared to be heretical." And provided this be done, "every thing is then," you say, "as it should be."

So that, in your opinion, it is fit, that herefy should be punished with temporal penalties; only care should be taken, that what is herefy be first settled by proper authority*. But here the question occurs, What is proper authority? and where is it lodged? I suppose, Sir, you will place it either with the ecclesiastical governors, or with the legislature. But in the hands of

---

* The nature of herefy, in the scripture-sense of the word, I think, hath been very much mistaken. The heretics, whom, in the New Testament, we are directed to avoid, were not the humble, modest, and peaceable, tho' erroneous Christians, who adhered to the authority of Christ, and desired to know and do his will; but the proud, pragmatical, turbulent party-men, who disturbed and divided the church by their impositions, and innovations in the terms of brotherly affection and Christian communion, and by assuming an authority over their fellow Christians. Herefy,

LETTER II.

of either, it will certainly amount to nothing more than human authority, the authority of fallible men; which, I apprehend, upon examination, will be found to be no authority at all in the present case, that is, in defining what is true faith, and what is heresy, and marking out their respective boundaries.

If the scripture is to determine for us, the point, I think, is clearly decided. For our blessed Saviour hath commanded his disciples not to be " called masters; for," saith he, " one is your Master, even Christ, " and all ye are brethren *;" and this he said in opposition to the authority which

---

resy, in the sense of scripture, doth not consist in simple error; nor were those heretics, who were anathematized and persecuted; but only those who anathematized and persecuted others, refusing to acknowledge them for true Christians, on account of their supposed or real mistakes. Whosoever carefully and conscientiously consults the sacred oracles, with a desire of knowing and doing the will of Christ, cannot be an heretic in the scripture-meaning of the expression. See Hallet's Notes and Discourses, vol. 3. disc. ix. throughout, especially p. 390.

* Matth. xxiii. 8, 10.

the Jewish rabbies assumed, in deciding questions of their law. And the apostles, who certainly, if any persons, might have pretended to authority in matters of faith, declared, that they "had no dominion o- "ver the faith" of Christians; but were "only helpers of their joy *." They appealed to reason and conscience, and referred the final decision to every man's own private judgment: "We speak as unto "wise men; judge ye what we say †." The Bereans are commended for "search- "ing the scriptures" of the Old Testament "daily," to see "whether the things" which the apostles declared to them "were "so" as they reported ‡. And it is the duty of every Christian to endeavour, for himself, to understand the sacred oracles, as well as he is able, in the use of all the means and helps which Divine Providence puts in his power §.

---

* 2 Cor. i. 24.   † 1 Cor. x. 15.   ‡ Acts xvii. 11.

§ Human helps and assistances, while they are only employed to open and inform the understanding, are very desirable

Indeed, every man's private perſuaſion or belief, muſt be founded upon evidence propoſed to his *own mind;* and he cannot but believe, according as things appear to HIMSELF, not to others; to his own underſtanding, not to that of any other man. Conviction is always produced by the *light* which is ſtruck into the mind; and never by compulſion, or the force of human authority *.

But firable and uſeful. But human authority, ſitting in judgment on points of faith, and deciding caſes of hereſy, and controuling, without enlightening, our underſtandings, is a very different thing. There is, ſurely, ſufficient room for our receiving inſtruction and aſſiſtance in matters of religion, without being deprived of our right of judging, in the laſt reſort, for ourſelves. And that we muſt do in oppoſition to all human authority, in whatſoever hands it be lodged, and with whatſoever venerable titles it comes recommended; or elſe we violate our allegiance to Chriſt, the only lawgiver and king in his church.

* If it be urged, that we believe many things upon *human authority:* I admit it, in caſe by authority we mean *teſtimony.* But there is a manifeſt difference between human teſtimony, as to matters of fact; and human authority, as to matters of opinion, and principles of truth. The former may be, and often is, a rational ground of belief; the latter

But it may be alledged, perhaps, that other mens underſtandings are better, and more penetrating and judicious than ours; or, that great numbers, eſpecially of perſons venerable for their age, as well as for their piety and learning, are more likely to be in the right, than a few individuals; and that, conſequently, it will be *ſafer* to be guided by their judgments than by our own. To this I reply: That a man's own underſtanding, be it more or leſs judicious, is the only faculty which God hath given him to diſtinguiſh truth from error: and as every man is accountable only for the

---

ter is believing upon no evidence, and is a renunciation of reaſon. The authority or teſtimony of the apoſtles, and firſt teachers of Chriſtianity, was accompanied with divine credentials; and this rendered it a ſufficient foundation for the belief, both of the facts and doctrines they revealed. And, indeed, human teſtimony, under the influence of inſpiration, and ſupported by miraculous interpoſition, is *always* a juſt ground of our belief of religious truth, as well as facts; but the authoritative decrees and injunctions of fallible, uninſpired men, *never*. The former claim an abſolute regard, as being a proof and evidence of a divine miſſion; the latter are no evidences of religious truth, or ground of belief of it at all, and therefore deſerve no regard.

use of his own understanding, not for that of other mens; consequently, his safety consists, not in giving up his own to the direction and controul of others, but in using it himself to the best advantage. And should he, in the careful and conscientious use of it, err; that error will never be imputed to him as a crime: Whereas, if he follow the judgment of other men, though ever so wise and learned, contrary to his own sense of things, he may perchance *profess* what is *right*, but he *does* what is *wrong*, and is highly criminal in the sight of God. For, the profession of any doctrine should always follow conviction of the truth of it; at least, a man must never profess what is contrary to his conviction. To embrace, or profess, any point which he does not believe to be true, in compliment to human authority, is exalting *human* into the place of *divine* authority; and saying in one word, That it is better to obey man than God.

So that for any man, or body of men,

whether clergy or laity, to assume an authority, first, to define what is heresy; and then to condemn and punish it by temporal penalties, is the ready way to make men hypocrites; while it can, in no case, render them true believers or good men *. But not to insist upon this: what I would principally observe to you, Sir, who are by profession a lawyer, is:

That heresy not being sufficiently defined by our laws, seems to be no small security, in connection with the lenity of the times, that those laws will not be executed; on account of the difficulty of defining what

---

* Submitting to the decisions of human authority in matters of faith, is sometimes prejudicial to, and even subversive of, true religion, where it does not issue in downright hypocrisy. For as, on the one hand, by the exercise of our rational faculties in searching after truth, we are not only likely to arrive at it, but to improve in the love of it, in candor, docility, and openness to conviction; and are disposed to submit to its influence: so, on the contrary, in proportion as we resign ourselves to the conduct of human authority, truth loses its charms, and its influence over us; and we become blind to its clearest evidences, and brightest characters, and are thus prepared to be led into the most absurd superstitions, and vilest corruptions of religion.

is

is herefy; and, perhaps, of finding a jury that will be forward in defining it, where the law hath left it doubtful and undefined. What, therefore, you, Sir, imagine a defect in the law, which ought to be supplied, appears to me to be a circumstance very favourable to the secure enjoyment of the rights of conscience; and, I hope, criminal prosecutions for opinion, either in civil or ecclesiastical courts, will never be rendered more easy and feasible, than they are at present.

The next enquiry, on supposition herefy is cognizable and punishable by human authority, (as you seem to think) naturally is: What that punishment shall be?

You tell us, that, " under these restric-" tions" (namely, that herefy should be more strictly defined; and no prosecution permitted, till the herefy is by proper authority ascertained) " it seems necessary, " for the support of the national religion, " that the officers of the church should " have

"have power to censure heretics, but not to exterminate or destroy them *." In this assertion is it not plainly supposed, that the censures of the church are to be attended with temporal penalties? only not so as to exterminate or destroy the heretic. In the name of humanity, Sir, is this the only exception to the extent and effect of the church's censures, that they shall not reach to utter extermination? Are all other pains and penalties proper, in whatsoever degree they are inflicted, which affect only a man's liberty or property, provided he is not destroyed thereby? If this be your meaning, (and, I think, you should have left no ground for suspicion that it is your meaning, if it is not) what more ample scope could any persecutor desire for his wanton cruelty, than you allow; unless, like another Bonner, he thirsted for human blood?—Excuse me, Sir, the warmth of my expression. This sentence of yours must, surely, have dropt from you

---

* Comment. vol. iv. p. 49.

you inadvertently; and can never seriously be intended to mean, what it seems to imply.

To examine the point more thoroughly: Is the infliction of temporal penalties upon heretics, really necessary to the support of a national establishment? If so, how comes it to pass, that a national establishment is in its nature so opposite to the genius of Christianity, of that kingdom which is not of this world, and which consists not in any thing this world can bestow or secure, but only in righteousness, truth, and peace? Religion is seated in the heart of man, and conversant with the inward principles and temper of the mind; and it cannot, therefore, properly speaking, be established by human laws, or enforced by temporal punishments. There is nothing in a fine, or a dungeon, or in any other penalty which the magistrate can inflict, that is calculated to produce conviction. Truth can only be supported and propagated by reason and argument; in conjunction with that mild and perfuasive infinuation, and that opennefs and candor, and apparent benevolence in its advocates, which are fuited to invite mens attention, and difpofe them to examination. No civil punifhments are adapted to enlighten the underftanding, or to conciliate the affections. And therefore the " weapons" which the minifters of religion (or, in your ftile, " the officers of " the church") are directed to ufe " are " not carnal *," but fpiritual.

For my own part, I believe, it would have fared much better with the intereft of true religion, if it had been left to make its way by the force of its own native excellence, and evidence only, than it hath done fince it hath been incorporated with civil conftitutions, and eftablifhed by human laws. For, even temporal emoluments, (leaving penalties out of the queftion) annexed to the profeffion of any

* 2 Cor. x. 4.

form

LETTER II.

form of religion, in such a degree as to excite mens avarice and ambition, and dispose them to mean and unworthy, not to say wicked compliances to obtain or secure them, have done, I apprehend, infinite mischief to the religious and moral characters of multitudes in all ages and countries.

But when such national establishments, besides the rewards which they bestow upon their church-officers, are guarded by temporal penalties, inflicted on all who cannot follow the lead of the publick wisdom and public conscience, they are then neither better nor worse than notorious violations of the laws of Christ, and of his royal prerogative; they are destructive of the very design of his religion, which is of no value if the profession and practice of it be not a free and reasonable service; and are an open invasion of the common rights of humanity.

But perhaps you will say, I am leading you into " a theological controver-
" sy

fy *." I shall only refer it, therefore, to your further confideration, whether the *law* cannot fupport the church in all her *rights* and *immunities*, unlefs fhe is invefted likewife with the unwarrantable and dangerous power of *punifhing* thofe who call in queftion, or diffent from her eftablifhed formularies of doctrine or worfhip.

If you only mean, indeed, by the cenfures of the church, her refufing communion to thofe who differ from her in articles of faith which fhe thinks important, without allowing her to inforce thofe cenfures by any temporal penalties; I acknowledge, I have then mifunderftood you. But I appeal to yourfelf, Sir, upon further reflection, whether that miftake, if it be one, is not owing to your affigning no other limitation to the effects of thofe cenfures, than that they fhould not extend to " utter extermination and deftruction."

* See Reply to Dr. Prieftley, p. 4.

I free-

I freely confess, I am so far from thinking, that any church hath a right to use temporal penalties to bring persons to her own terms of communion, that, I apprehend, she is invested with no authority to make any terms of communion at all, which Christ hath not made; and those which he hath made, are only to be enforced by spiritual sanctions; by his own authority as head of the church, by the dread of his displeasure, and by the hope of his favour. And a national church, I apprehend, will stand much firmer upon this noble and extensive foundation of reason and scripture, than on the narrow and feeble one of human authority, fenced, as much as you please, with all the terrors of pains and penalties.

Perhaps it will be asked, Are we to leave every man at liberty to propagate what sentiments he pleases? It is my opinion, I profess, that truth is so far from suffering by free examination, that this is

the

the only method in which she can be effectually supported and propagated. But, with this idea I am not so happy as to be able to reconcile the following sentiment: "I would not" you say "be understood to "derogate from the just rights of the na-"tional church, or to encourage a loose "latitude of propagating any crude undi-"gested sentiments in religious matters: "of propagating, I say; for the bare en-"tertaining them seems hardly cognisable "by any human authority *."

That indeed is very true; and a good reason there is for it, because the heart of man is inscrutable; because there is a *natural impossibility* for any human authority to interfere with the inward sentiments of the mind, while they are concealed from outward observation. But the moment they are declared, and reasons are offered in support or defence of them, human authority may interpose, it seems; because it is

* Comment, vol. iv. p. 49.

"one of the juſt rights of the national church, from which," you ſay, "you will by no means derogate," to prevent the propagation of any crude undigeſted ſentiments in religious matters:" that is in reality, (for to this it amounts) any ſentiments different from thoſe by law eſtabliſhed; every eſtabliſhment ſuppoſing thoſe ſentiments to be crude and undigeſted, which are contrary to its own principles and practices. A maxim, which will vindicate the exerciſe of human authority in ſupport of every eſtabliſhment that ever was, or will be: Mohammediſm at Conſtantinople, Popery at Rome, Epiſcopacy in England, Preſbyterianiſm at Geneva, or in Scotland! For all the adherents to theſe ſeveral perſuaſions think, thoſe who differ from them entertain, at leaſt, *crude and undigeſted ſentiments in religious matters.* Indeed, this principle, purſued into its genuine conſequences, would have precluded the Reformation from Popery, and would even have ſtifled in its birth our holy

holy religion itself. If the propagation of truth, or of supposed truth, in matters purely religious, is to be restrained by human authority, (whether you call it civil or ecclesiastical, is the same at last; for they are both alike exercised by fallible men): in that case, the success of true religion in the world, depends wholly on the power of the magistrate, or on the majority; either of which may be as likely, at least, to be on the side of error as of truth.

From this idea, that the suppression of heresy, or the preventing the propagation of it, by temporal penalties, is necessary to the establishment of truth, or of a church, have been derived all those execrable and outrageous persecutions which have disgraced not only our religion, but human nature itself. For there is a gradation, in this case, as natural as it is common; the same principle which induces men, at first, to employ what are called moderate penalties, in order to compass so good an end as the suppression

of

of error, leading them (in case that end cannot *otherwise* be accomplished, that end which they think *must* be accomplished: the very same principle, I say, leading them) to measures still more and more severe and intolerant, till by degrees they are reconciled to the most inhuman persecutions, and bloody massacres. And in case they do not proceed to such lengths, to what shall we ascribe it? to their principle? or to their humanity pleading against principle?

I am far, Sir, from insinuating, that you hold all the consequences which flow from the maxim you seem to entertain, namely, that temporal penalties may be employed in promoting truth and suppressing error: it is sufficient for me to observe, that all those positions must be erroneous, from which such consequences naturally follow.——I am, Sir, &c.

LETTER III.

SIR,

Though the reasoning in my last letter may be applied to the case of apostacy, as well as heresy; the case of renouncing Christianity, or professing Deism; yet as you have advanced some particular arguments for inflicting human punishment upon infidels, I shall take the liberty to give what you have offered a distinct consideration; because, I apprehend, it would be dishonourable to the Christian religion to be even suspected to owe its preservation, not to its own excellence and evidence and the special protection of Providence, but to the terror of penal laws, and the sword of the civil magistrate.

Having

LETTER III.

Having premifed, that " the lofs of life is a heavier penalty than the crime of apoftacy deferves;" you remark, that, about the clofe of the laft century, the civil liberties to which we were then reftored being ufed as a cloke of malicioufnefs, and the moft horrid doctrines fubverfive of all religion being publickly avowed both in difcourfe and writings, it was found neceffary again," (the punifhment of death for this crime being become obfolete) " for the civil power to interpofe, by not admitting thefe mifcreants" (explained in the margin by *mefcroyantz*, the French word ufed in our ancient laws for unbelievers) " to the privileges of fociety, who maintained fuch principles as deftroyed all moral obligation. " To this end," you fay, " it was enacted by ftatute 9 & 10 Will. III. c. 32, that if any perfon educated in, or having made profeffion of, the Chriftian religion, fhall, by writing, printing, teaching, or advifed fpeaking, deny the Chriftian religion

"gion to be true, or the holy scriptures to
"be of divine authority, he shall, for the
"first offence, be rendered incapable to hold
"any office or place of trust; and, for the
"second, be rendered incapable of bringing
"any action, being guardian, executor,
"legatee, or purchaser of lands, and shall
"suffer three years imprisonment without
"bail:" the same penalties, which have been already mentioned, as by this very statue inflicted on Arianism.— And you had just before observed, that "all affronts
"to Christianity, or endeavours to depre-
"ciate its efficacy, are highly deserving of
"human punishment*."

I have already shown, that principles or sentiments relating to religion are not punishable by penal laws. The infliction of such punishment, even when they are professed, is out of the magistrate's province; as, when they are concealed, it is out of

* Comment. vol. iv. p. 44.

LETTER III.

his power; for human laws have nothing to do with mere principles, but only with those overt acts arising from them, which are contrary to the peace and good order of society.

But it will be said, Hath the magistrate no concern with those principles which "destroy the foundation of moral obliga-"tion?" that is, if I understand you right, which have a *tendency* to introduce immorality and licentiousness.

I allow, he may encourage, amongst all sects, those general principles of religion and morality, on which the happiness of society depends. This he may, and should do, as *conservator* of the publick weal. But with regard to the belief or disbelief of religious principles, or religious systems, if he presumes to exercise his *authority* as a *judge*, in such cases, with a view of restraining and punishing those who embrace and profess what he dislikes, or dislike and explode what he embraces, on account of the supposed ill tendency of their principles.

ciples, he goes beyond his province, which is confined to those effects of such principles, that is, to those actions, which affect the peace and good order of society; and every step he takes, he is in danger of trampling on the rights of conscience, and of invading the prerogative of the only arbiter of conscience, to whom alone men are accountable for professing, or not professing, religious sentiments and principles.

For, if the magistrate be possessed of a power to restrain and punish any principles relating to religion because of their tendency, and he be the judge of that tendency; as he must be, if he be vested with authority to punish on that account; religious liberty is entirely at an end; or, which is the same thing, is under the controul, and at the mercy of the magistrate, according as he shall think the tenets in question affect the foundation of moral obligation, or are favourable or unfavourable to religion and morality. But, if the line be drawn
between

between mere religious principle and the tendency of it, on the one hand; and those overt acts which affect the publick peace and order, on the other; and if the latter alone be assigned to the jurisdiction of the magistrate, as being guardian of the peace of society in this world, and the former, as interfering only with a future world, be reserved to a man's own conscience, and to God, the only sovereign Lord of conscience; the boundaries between civil power and liberty, in religious matters, are clearly marked and determined; and the latter will not be wider or narrower, or just nothing at all, according to the magistrate's opinion of the good or bad tendency of principles.

If it be objected, that when the tendency of principles is unfavourable to the peace and good order of society, as it may be, it is the magistrate's duty then, and for that reason, to restrain them by penal laws: I reply, that the tendency of principles, though it be *unfavourable*, is not *prejudicial* to society, till it issues in some *overt acts* against the publick peace and order; and when it does, *then* the magistrate's authority to punish commences; that is, he may punish the *overt acts,* but not the *tendency,* which is not actually hurtful; and, therefore, his penal laws should be directed against *overt acts only,* which are detrimental to the peace and good order of society, let them spring from what principle they will; and not against *principles,* or the *tendency* of principles.

The distinction between the tendency of principles, and the overt acts arising from them, is, and cannot but be, observed in many cases of a *civil* nature; in order to determine the bounds of the magistrate's power, or at least to limit the exercise of of it, in such cases. It would not be difficult to mention customs and manners, as well as principles, which have a tendency unfavourable to society; and which, nevertheless, cannot be restrained by penal laws, except with the total destruction of civil

civil liberty. And here, the magistrate must be contented with pointing his penal laws against the evil overt acts resulting from them. In the same manner he should act in regard to mens professing, or rejecting, religious principles or systems. Punishing a man for the *tendency* of his principles, is punishing him *before* he is guilty, for fear he *should be* guilty.

Besides, if the magistrate in one country hath a right to punish those who reject the religion which is there publickly professed, the magistrates of all other countries must have the same right; and for the same reason, namely, to guard against the evil tendency of renouncing a religion, the maitenance of which they think of great importance to society. If those persons who reject Christianity are to be punished in England, those who embrace it are to be punished in Turkey. This is the necessary consequence of allowing any penal laws to be enacted, and to operate, in support or suppression of any religious system;

for

for the magistrate must and will use his power according to his own religious persuasion.

If it be said, that punishment is not to be inflicted on the mere entertaining, but only on the zealous propagating, of the principles of infidelity; it should be considered, that the propagation of Christianity would, on this maxim, be obstructed, and even precluded, where a different religion already prevails, by making it the duty of the magistrate to oppose it, and punish those who attempt it.

But having asserted, that "all affronts " to Christianity, or endeavours to depre- " ciate its efficacy, are highly deserving of " human punishment," or punishment from the magistrate, you endeavour to prove your position by the following observation: That " the belief of a future " state of rewards and punishments, the " entertaining just ideas of the moral at- " tributes of the supreme Being, and a
" firm

LETTER III.

"firm persuasion that he superintends, and will finally compensate, every action in human life, (all which are clearly revealed in the doctrines, and forcibly inculcated by the precepts, of our Saviour Christ) these are the grand foundation of all judicial oaths, which call God to witness the truth of those facts which perhaps may be only known to him and the party attesting. All moral evidence, therefore, all confidence in human veracity," you say, "must be weakened by irreligion, and overthrown by infidelity *."

If by infidelity you mean disbelief of Christianity, then it will be a fair inference from this last assertion, that there can be no human faith, no mutual confidence, no bond of society, and no civil government, in countries which are not Christian. But the fact is otherwise; and the reason is, because there are some principles of re-

* Comment. vol. iv. p. 43, 44.

ligion

ligion and morality prevailing even in Mohammedan and heathen countries; and those right principles, though greatly short of a religious system, and blended with many erroneous, absurd, superstitious principles; yet, have sufficient influence in general on the minds of those who embrace them, to answer, tolerably at least, the purposes of civil government, and of mutual confidence and commerce.

I admit, that, provided every one who revolts from Christianity to Deism renounced, together with his former profession, all those principles of natural religion on which the obligation of judicial oaths is founded, (and possibly you understand infidelity in this extensive sense, when you speak of its " overthrowing all human " confidence"): if, I say, he were known to have renounced these principles, your argument would be *so far* good, that his oath would deserve no credit, and he would be subjected to innumerable inconveniencies and incapacities, which his being

ing destitute of the firm confidence of other men, and being discredited in his judicial oaths, would naturally and necessarily bring upon him: and indeed, such an absolute infidel as to all religion, natural as well as revealed, if proved to be so, should not be admitted to take an oath in a court of judicature. But as for inflicting any *positive punishment* upon him, merely for rejecting right *principles,* or espousing wrong ones, while this does not issue in those *actions* which call for punishment; *that*, I think, for the reasons already assigned, is beyond the province and jurisdiction of the magistrate.

In what I have just now said, I have supposed these unbelievers of Christianity to reject the great principles of natural as well as revealed religion; which, you rightly tell us, are the grand foundation of all judicial oaths. But the truth is, many who profess not to believe revelation, may possibly believe those principles as firmly as some nominal Christians, whose depositions

depositions on oath are not scrupled in courts of judicature. The belief of a God, the moral governor of the world, the searcher of hearts, the infallible judge, rewarder and punisher of human actions, is, as you observe, the only foundation of a judicial oath; and if men *do believe* these articles, they should not be made liable to that punishment, which, on your own state of the case, is due only to those who *do not* believe them; they should not be punished, I say, when they *do* believe them, merely because they believe them upon reasons independent of their "being " clearly revealed in the doctrines of " Christ;" for their believing them is all that your argument requires.

Indeed, we have a ceremony in administering a judicial oath, which supposes a belief of the Christian religion. But that is by no means a necessary, essential part of a solemn judicial appeal to heaven; and can afford, therefore, no plea for punishing those who do not believe Christianity,

LETTER III.

as incapable of a judicial oath, (suppoſing that a proper reaſon for puniſhment); becauſe it is obvious, the end may be anſwered by an appeal to God in ſome other ſolemn form, without this ceremony; and our laws have ſet an example of it in the caſe of the Quakers.

If it be enquired, whether men ſhall be ſuffered with impunity to " *affront* Chri-" ſtianity, and depreciate its efficacy," by reproaches and calumnies, offenſive to every Chriſtian; a different caſe from ſimply diſbelieving or modeſtly oppoſing it: I anſwer, that, provided it be unwarrantable to ſupport the belief of Chriſtianity, and to confute its oppoſers, by penal laws and the ſword of the magiſtrate, its profeſſors ſhould be exceeding tender how they animadvert, in this way, on the *manner* in which the oppoſition to it is made: a thing, comparatively, of little conſequence. For, though calumny and ſlander, when affecting our fellow-men, are puniſhable by law;

law; for this plain reason, because an injury is done, and a damage sustained, and a reparation therefore due to the injured party; yet, this reason cannot hold where God and the Redeemer are concerned; who can sustain no injury from low malice and scurrilous invective, nor can any reparation be made to them by temporal penalties; for these can work no conviction or repentance in the mind of the offender; and if he continue impenitent and incorrigible, he will receive his condign punishment in the day of final retribution. Affronting Christianity, therefore, does not come under the magistrate's cognizance, in this particular view, as it implies an offence against God and Christ.

If you say, that insulting and reviling religion is very offensive to good men, and ought, on that account, to be prohibited and punished: I observe, so are all transgressions of the divine law, very offensive to good men; but they are not, for that reason, all punishable by the magistrate.

In

LETTER III. 63

In the case of gross lying, heinous ingratitude, and many other vices which might be mentioned, though no one thinks of applying to a court of justice on the occasion, yet every good man will treat these vices, and those who are guilty of them, with just abhorrence and detestation. And the same, and no other, I apprehend, should be their conduct, when infidels, with an offensive indecency, vent their impotent rancour against the religion of Jesus.

If you alledge, that this licentious manner of treating religion, will " depreciate its " efficacy" on the minds of men, especially of the undiscerning and thoughtless, which are commonly the major part: I answer, that the contempt and abuse which infidels throw upon religion, will, in the end, entail disgrace and infamy on themselves. Their ribaldry and scurrility will be despicable and disgustful to the more sensible part of our species; and while there are Christians, especially Christian ministers,

in

in the world, I truft, there will always be proper perfons, who will expofe to the moft ignorant and unreflecting, the grofs folly and injuftice of fuch abufe, and renthofe who are guilty of it the objects of contempt to the loweft of the people: whereas, if punifhed by the magiftrate, they would be the objects, probably, of their pity: a circumftance which would procure their infinuations and fuggeftions to the prejudice of religion a much more favourable reception, than they would otherwife be like to obtain.

Indeed, difcovering a difpofition to take refuge in temporal penalties, whenever any perfons in difcourfe or writings mifreprefent and revile (or, as you ftile it, *affront*) our holy religion, and depreciate its efficacy, is acting as if we apprehended the caufe had no other and better fupport. Whereas, for three hundred years after its firft promulgation, Chriftianity maintained its full reputation and influence, (though attacked in every way which wit or malice

lice could invent) not only without the affiftance of, but in direct oppofition to the civil power. It fhone with the brighter luftre, for the attempts to eclipfe it. And the infults and calumnies of its enemies were as ineffectual to its prejudice, as either their objections, or, what were more to be feared, their perfecutions. And as it was during that period, fo will it always be, if there be any ground to rely on that promife of our bleffed Saviour concerning his church, that " the gates of " hell fhall not prevail againft it *."

In the mean time, compaffion to all ignorant, petulant, malicious adverfaries of our holy religion; and a defire to obviate the mifchief they do, by refuting their arguments, expofing their petulance and malice, and if poffible, working conviction in their minds; are the difpofitions which fuch contemptible attacks on the honour of the Chriftian religion, and its author, fhould excite in his ge-

* Matth. xvi. 18.

nuine disciples. We should argue with such men, not persecute them; should endeavour to rescue others from the danger of being infected by their principles, with cool reasoning; but we should be careful how we attempt to punish them, lest we *harden* instead of reclaiming them: lest we leave room for others to imagine, that not their scoffs and insults, but their *arguments*, have *provoked us* by being unanswerable. And indeed, provided it be wrong to animadvert, by temporal penalties, on the calm reasoning of infidels against Christianity; it would, surely, be *imprudent* to punish them for what renders their arguments, if there be any, less formidable and prejudicial; I mean, their revilings and their scurrility. It is *imprudent*, I say, by a prosecution, to hold up to publick notice, to introduce into all conversation, and excite peoples curiosity after, those scurrilous writings, which would otherwise quickly sink with their authors into perpetual oblivion. Many infidels,

infidels, in modern times, have united their efforts against the Christian religion; and they have railed, at least some of them, much more than they have reasoned; but they have been heard, and confuted; and most of them are only remembered by the excellent apologies for Christianity, which they have been the occasions of producing. I hardly think they and their works would have been so soon forgotten; I am sure, our religion would not have received such honour, nor infidelity such disgrace, and such a total defeat, if, instead of being answered by the learned writers, who have employed their abilities to so laudable a purpose, they had been prosecuted, fined, imprisoned, or suffered any other ignominious or cruel punishment, by sentence of the magistrate. Those who call for the aid of the civil power, and for the infliction of pains and penalties, in support of the Christian religion, forget the character and conduct of its divine author; who, when his apostles, out of zeal for his honour, would have invoked fire from heaven on the unbelieving Samaritans, becaufe they had juft *affronted* him, feverely rebuked them :. " Ye know not " what manner of fpirit ye are of; the Son " of man came not to deftroy mens lives, " but to fave them *."

In what I have faid, let it not be fuppofed, that I have pleaded the caufe of infidelity. No; I have pleaded that of Chriftianity, in my own opinion at leaft; the mild and forbearing fpirit of which religion, I defire more and more to imbibe, to regard all its doctrines and precepts as the rule of my faith and manners, its promifes as the foundation of my hopes, and the fcheme of redemption through Jefus Chrift as my higheft confolation and joy. It is, indeed, from my reverence for it, and attachment to it, and zeal for its true dignity and honour, that I will ever vindicate it from the *leaft fufpicion* of being a

* Luke ix. 55, 56.

perfecuting

persecuting religion *: A suspicion, which, if it were just, would be a greater brand of ignominy, and do it more real discredit, than all the invidious misrepresentations and calumnies of its adversaries. And this

---

* Several writers of the first rank amongst those who have appeared in defence of Christianity, have declared openly, and argued strongly, against the persecution of infidels: particularly Dr. Lardner, in his preface to his excellent " Vindication of three miracles of our Saviour " against Woolston; and in two " Letters to the Bishop of " Chichester," published in the late " Memoirs of his " life:" Dr. Chandler, in his preface to the " Conduct " of the modern deists:" and Mr. Simon Brown, in his preface to a very shrewd and sensible pamphlet against Woolston, which he stiles " A fit rebuke to a ludicrous in- " fidel." The performances of these writers shew, that they perfectly *understood* the strength of their cause; and their aversion to the interposition of the civil power, that they altogether *relied* upon it, having no apprehensions of the consequences of a free debate, managed in any way the patrons of infidelity should think proper. Indeed, no one ever made the attack in a more rude and scurrilous manner than Woolston: they, however, contented them- selves with confuting his arguments and exposing his scurri- lity, entering their protest, with convincing reasons, against the prosecution of him. And this conduct I cannot help thinking very much to the honour of the Christian religion and its advocates.

it becomes those seriously to consider, who would wipe away the dishonour done it, by methods that would double the disgrace, not only on themselves, but on the noble cause which they profess to espouse.
——I am, Sir, &c.

LETTER IV.

SIR,

WHEN you mention the statute 1 Eliz. c. 2. which enacts, that "if "any person whatsoever shall, in plays, "songs, or other open words, speak any "thing in derogation, depraving, or de- "spising of the common prayer, he shall "forfeit for the first offence an hundred "marks, for the second offence four hun- "dred, and for the third offence shall for- "feit all his goods and chattels, and suf- "fer imprisonment for life:" I say, when you speak of this statute, you not only approve of it in the peculiar circumstances of the time when it was first enacted; but you say, that "the continuance of it to "the present time cannot be thought too severe or intolerant*." And the reason you assign is, that "no one in the present circumstances can do this," that is, "revile" the liturgy (the crime to which alone you suppose the act to refer) "from any laudable motive, not even from a mistaken zeal for reformation; it being, since the union, extremely unadvisable to make any alterations in the established church †."

Now, supposing that a man cannot have any "laudable motive for reviling and inveighing with bitterness against the common prayer," (for against this only, I say, you understand the act to be levelled): supposing it to be a thing very culpable; yet, what is the specific nature of the crime, and wherein doth the malignity of it consist? "It is a crime," you say, "of a grosser nature than mere nonconfor-

* Comment. vol. iv. p. 50, 51.
† This argument against alterations, taken from the union, will be considered particularly in a subsequent letter.

"mity;

LETTER IV. 73

"mity: because it carries with it the ut-
"most indecency, arrogance, and ingrati-
"tude: indecency, by setting up private
"judgment in opposition to public; arro-
"gance, by treating with contempt and
"rudeness what hath at least a better
"chance to be right, than the singular no-
"tions of any particular man; and ingra-
"titude, by denying that indulgence and
"liberty of conscience to the members of
"the national church, which the retainers
"to every petty conventicle * enjoy †."

This crime of reviling the liturgy, I perceive, is a very complicated one; "it car-
"ries with it," you say, "the utmost in-
"decency, arrogance, and ingratitude."
For each of which you assign a particular

---

* Dr. Priestley hath remarked a want of elegance and po-
liteness in this expression, unworthy of a fine writer, (Remarks, p. 52, 53.): I would observe an impropriety in it,
unbecoming the great lawyer. The word conventicle, if I
understand it right, means an unlawful assembly; and is
therefore improperly applied, as it is here, to the legal af-
semblies of Protestant Dissenters.

† Comment. vol. iv. p. 50.

reason;

reason; and I shall examine them all in their order.

That reviling any thing, that treating with rudeness and contempt any man, much more a considerable body of men, or the publick at large, or those religious forms which are used under the sanction of authority, and by many revered, is *indecent*, will be readily allowed. The rules of civility and good manners ought always to be observed; especially where the publick, and persons in authority, are concerned. Never to violate them, if possible, is in itself right; and is also good policy; for any cause, instead of being disserved, will be recommended and promoted, by being defended with civility and good temper.

But I cannot help suspecting, Sir, that your view reaches further than this; if this be all you mean, I do not conceive why the indecency of reviling the liturgy is, particularly, said to arise from " set-
" ting up private judgment in opposition
" to

LETTER IV.

"to publick:" I say, your putting the indecency of it on this footing, appears to me to be accounted for only by supposing, that you think it wrong to oppose private to publick judgment, in any case; and then nonconformity and reviling the liturgy are both indecent; for the same reason, because they are an opposition of the private to the public judgment; only one is more so than the other, and consequently more indecent. And I the rather apprehend I am herein not very wide of your sentiment, because you do consider nonconformity as a crime, though not so great as that of reviling the liturgy; and you so consider it, I imagine, on this particular account, as it is private judgment opposed to the publick.

And indeed, if it be a general maxim, that it is *indecent* to " set up private judg-
" ment in opposition to publick;" then it is certainly so, to dissent from publick or established opinions and practices: then all those who have been the authors of any

refor-

reformations or improvements, in religion, in philosophy*, in policy, and in the manners and conduct of life, contrary to the publick standard, have been guilty of indecency.

Besides, it is worth observation, that the publick judgment, to which it is expected

---

* The *publick judgment* of the church of Rome hath condemned for heresy the doctrine of the motion of the earth according to the system of Copernicus; notwithstanding which it hath long passed for orthodoxy in the *private judgment* of all philosophers. The famous Galileo, having taught this point, and confirmed it by new discoveries, was imprisoned in the Inquisition on that account, obliged to recant and curse his former opinion, and swear that he would not teach it any more; but that if he should know of any such heretic, or any person suspected of such heresy, he would immediately report him to the holy office. Such a fatal operation had this *publick judgment* formerly, in a point of *philosophy*, capable of demonstration, and now universally received. And the influence of it, though it be privately rejected by every individual, appears in the publick *profession* of philosophers even in modern times. Two learned Jesuits and able mathematicians, publishing an edition of Sir Isaac Newton's Principia, with an excellent Commentary, in which his principles are explained and more fully demonstrated, (the *monitum* or advertisement to the third book of which is dated at Rome 1742), thought it necessary, for their safety I suppose, before they entered upon the

pected such deference should be paid, amounts to no more than the vote of those who happen to be invested with power, at the time such establishments are made; which is sometimes very different from the opinion or judgment of the publick at *that time*, and frequently differs widely from the judgment of the publick in a *subsequent period*. But the unhappiness is,

the heretical doctrine De systemate mundi, to make, in form, the following curious declaration; than which, however it was designed, there never surely was a greater burlesque upon servile submission to publick judgment.

P. P. Le Seur & Jacquier declaratio.

Newtonus, in hoc tertio libro, telluris motæ hypothesim assumit. Autoris propositiones aliter explicari non poterant, nisi eâdem quoque factâ hypothesi. Hinc alienam coacti sumus gerere personam. Cæterum latis à summis Pontificibus contra telluris motum decretis obsequi profitemur.

The declaration of the fathers Le Seur and Jacquier.

Newton, in this third book, assumes the hypothesis of the earth's motion. The author's propositions could not be explained, if we did not also go upon the same hypothesis. Upon this account we have been obliged to appear under a feigned character. We profess, however, to follow the decrees issued by the sovereign Pontiffs against the motion of the earth.

that,

that, when the thing eftablifhed, be it what it will, hath received the fanction of publick authority, neither numbers, nor the refpectable characters of thofe who difapprove it, can eafily procure a reform; and even when it is in a manner grown out of all credit, fo as to be efpoufed by very few, it ftill paffes under the denomination of "the publick judgment," againft which it is "indecency to oppofe the private judgment" of individuals *.

But fince a man's private judgment *may happen* to be in the right, and the publick one in the wrong; whenever this is found, or generally agreed, to be the cafe, he muft make but an aukward figure who gravely reprimands thofe that fet up the former againft the latter. I fhould think it, therefore, much better to come to the

---

* If the Athanafian creed, with its damnatory claufes, were now a candidate for admiffion into the publick formulary, it would doubtlefs be rejected by a very large majority, both of clergy and laity; and yet it remains one of thofe things which are authorifed by the *publick judgment*.

queftion

question at once: Is the thing in deliberation right or wrong? for the opinion, neither of men in power, nor of the majority, is the test of truth, or the rule of our faith or practice.

So that the particular reason on which you ground the " indecency of reviling the " liturgy," namely, that it is " setting up " private judgment in opposition to pu- " blick," appears to me to be very inadequate and unsatisfactory.

The next article in the composition of this crime, namely, reviling the common prayer, is, you say, " arrogance." It is " arrogant to treat with rudeness and con- " tempt what hath a better chance to be " right, than the singular notions of any " particular man."

In using the phrase, " the singular no- " tions of a particular man," you put the case very favourably for drawing your own conclusion. To be sure, if a man adopts sentiments which never entered into any body's body's head but his own, or which no one will embrace when proposed, the odds are against him. But this is not often the case; and is not so, in particular, with regard to the debate between the church and the Dissenters, the point here in question. However, he who treats the notions of others with a rude contempt, does, I think, in most cases, appear to affect a sort of superiority, (call it arrogance, or insolence, if you please), which usually ill becomes him who assumes it, and is never very agreeable to those who are the objects of it.

But with relation to the query, Who have the fairest chance of being in the right? those who follow the lead of a publick establishment? or those who are, or profess to be, impartial enquirers after truth? that, I think, is not so clear, at least on one side of the question, as you seem to imagine.— Most establishments, even those which have been settled by authority of the civil power, have originated

LETTER IV.

ginated from the clergy; at least, with respect to their formularies of doctrine and worship; and the magistrate hath had little more to do in the affair, than to establish what hath been already prepared to his hands. Let us, then, look into ecclesiastical history, and see what the councils, synods, convocations, and other general, national, or provincial assemblies of the clergy, have, for the most part, been, from the first famous and revered council of Nice, down to the last session of our own convocation in England. When I reflect on the policy and artifice used in the management of such assemblies; on their obsequiousness to the caprices of princes, and ministers of state, or of potent ecclesiastics, and even of some of their own ambitious and turbulent members; on their prejudices and passions, their private and party views, their scandalous animosities and contentions; on the small majorities by which questions of importance, intended to bind not only the men of

that

that age but their posterity, have been determined*; on the respectable characters which have often appeared in the minor number †; and above all, on their self-contra-

---

* The cross in baptism, and kneeling at the communion, (which are imposed in the church of England as necessary to the administration of these ordinances) as well as the observation of saints days, and a few other ceremonies, were carried in the convocation of Elizabeth 1562 by a single proxy. The majority of those present, *against* them, was 43 against 35; but upon adding the proxies, the majority, *for* them, was 59 against 58. Thus they obtained the honour of the *publick judgment* by this *better chance of being in the right*; and the contrary opinion was degraded into *private judgment*, though hardly so as to become the *singular notion of a particular man*. Strype's Annals, vol. i. p. 337,—339. edit. 3. Burnet's History of the Reformation, vol. iii. No. 74. among the Records, p. 662,—664. edit. 1753.

† King William, in the first year of his reign, granted a commission to prepare alterations of the liturgy and canons, and proposals for the reformation of the ecclesiastical courts. In this commission, besides several others, there were such men as Tillotson, Stillingfleet, Burnet, Patrick, Tennison, Lloyde, Sharp, Kidder, Scot, Fowler. And they accordingly made very considerable alterations and improvements in the liturgy; which are highly commended by Dr. Nichols, in his *Defensio Ecclesiæ Anglicanæ*, p. 94, to 97. and which Mr. Neal, in his *History of the Puritans*, saith,

LETTER IV.

contradictions, and their mutual censures and anathemas *: I say, when I consider these things, I own, they somewhat abate my reverence for the determinations of such bodies,

faith, would, if they had been adopted, have brought in three parts in four of the Dissenters, vol. ii. p. 804. edit. 4to. And this author was a good judge, since no one better understood their principles and dispositions. However, the convocation, when the matter was laid before them by a message from the crown, resolved to enter into no debates about alterations, would return no answer to that part of the King's message, and could hardly be brought to thank him for his promise of protection. Burnet's History of his own Times, under the year 1689. In what a contemptible light does that majority in convocation appear, who would not so much as *hear* what was prepared for their consideration by *such celebrated divines*, the glory of the English church, acting under a royal commission! and who would not esteem it an honour to be found in such a minority! and yet their sentiments, outvoted by furious bigots, are now only *private judgment!*

* A few remarks upon the four first general councils, will be a sufficient illustration of what is here said. The council of Nice, we are told, consisted of more than 300 bishops, " brought together, some by the hope of gain, and others " to see such a miracle of an emperor as Constantine;" who accordingly well rewarded them " by his presents as well as " his entertainments." Euseb. in vit. Const. l. 3. c. 6. & 16. Sozom. l. 1. c. 25. p. 42. Theodorit. l. 1. c. 11. p. 36.

Sabinus

bodies, and for the establishments founded by them, or by the civil power in consequence of their resolves; and I am apt to surmise, that a candid enquirer after truth would

Sabinus saith, that "they were weak and illiterate men," (vid. Socrat. l. 1. c. 8. p. 21. & c. 9. p. 31.); which might be true with regard to many of them. However, it is certain, all history agreeing in it, that they were in general (πολλοι, πλειονες are the words of Socrates and Sozomen) very litigious and contentious; insomuch that the emperor was obliged to interpose, to take them off from their private quarrels, and from their daily custom of presenting to him accusations against one another, before he could get them to attend to the business for which they were called together, (Euseb. de vit. Constant. l. 3. c. 13. Socrat. l. 1. c 8. p. 20. Sozom. l. 1. c. 17. p. 35. Theodorit. l. 1. c. 11. p. 37. Gelasius Cyzic. l. 2. c. 8.); and when they did engage in it, their conduct was agreeable to their character; for the party accused having laid before them a written confession of their faith, they immediately tore it in pieces; and a great tumult arising, and those who presented the paper, being cried out upon as betrayers of the faith, were so terrified, that they all arose, except two, and were the first in condemning the sentiments and party they before espoused, Theodorit, l. 1. c. 7. p. 27. With such violence were matters carried in the council! And the unintelligible terms which they introduced into their creeds and definitions of faith, and imposed by dint of authority upon others, only served to increase and perpetuate the controversies then subsisting, and fill the world with mutual rage

and

would esteem it a much fairer chance for being in the right, to follow his own judgment, or, if any other, the judgment of a few serious, impartial, disinterested enquirers,

and mutual persecution. " The consequence of which " was, that the Christian religion, which, for 300 years " after the ascension of Jesus, had been spreading over a " large part of Asia, Europe, and Africa, without the as- " sistance of secular power and church-authority, and at the " convening of the council of Nice, was almost every where " through those countries in a flourishing condition, in the " space of another 300 years, or a little more, was great- " ly corrupted in a large part of that extent, its glory deba- " sed, and its light almost extinguished." Dr. Lardner's Credibil. vol. 8. p. 24. This council, we are informed by Socrates, l. 1. c. 11. p. 38, 39. by Sozomen, l. 1. c. 23. p. 41. and by Nicephorus Callistus, l. 8. c. 19. tom. 1. p. 571. was on the point of decreeing the celibacy of the clergy, if they had not been diverted from it by a spirited oration of Paphnutius, an Egyptian bishop; and perhaps by perceiving, that it was disagreeable to the emperor; as it probably was, if we may judge by the marks of singular respect which he shewed that bishop. Socrat. l. 1. c. 11. p. 38.

The next general council of Constantinople was called to confirm the decisions of the council of Nice, which had not in the least extinguished the rage of controversy. Previous to it, the emperor wrote to the inhabitants of that city, that he " would have all his subjects be of the same reli- " gion, which Peter, prince of the apostles, had from the " beginning delivered to the Romans, and which was now " held

quirers, like himself, than to adopt the resolutions of the most venerable synod, in which truth and right are decided by the major vote. I would not be thought

to

"held by Damasus, bishop of Rome, and Peter, bishop of
"Alexandria." Sozom. l. 7. c. 4. So respectable a father as Gregory Nazianzen, in a letter which he wrote to Procopius to excuse himself with the emperor from attending this council, saith, that he was "desirous of avoiding all sy-
"nods, because he had never seen a good effect, or happy
"conclusion of any one of them; that they rather increased
"than lessened the evils they were designed to prevent.
"For the love of contention, and lust of power, were there
"manifested in instances innumerable." Operum, tom. 1. p. 814. epist. 55. edit. Paris 1630. And what the good father said concerning former councils, not excepting the famous one of Nice, he found afterwards to be true of this council of Constantinople. "These conveyers of the Holy
"Ghost," saith he, "these preachers of peace to all men,
"grow so bitterly outrageous and clamorous against one
"another in the midst of the church, bandying into par-
"ties, mutually accusing each other, leaping about as if
"they had been mad, under the furious impulse of a lust
"of power and dominion, as if they would have rent the
"whole world in pieces." He saith afterwards, that "this
"was not the effect of piety, but of a contention for
"thrones:" ουκ ευσεβειας—την δ'υπερ θρονων εριν. And he gives a strange account of their indecent behaviour, when he had just made a speech to them. "These furious
"young men were followed by the elder," saith he,
"and

LETTER IV.

to be an advocate for an arrogant, infolent, pragmatical contempt of the opinions of others; what I mean is, that were I to be under direction in the purfuit of truth, I had

---

"and ruled the council." Greg. Naz. de vit. fua, operum tom. 2. p. 25, 27.

The general council of Ephefus was called on this occafion. Neftorius was of opinion, that the two natures in Chrift were not fo united after the incarnation, as to occafion a mutual communication of properties. He therefore objected to calling the Virgin Mary, Θεοτοκος, the mother of God; and would have her called, Χριστοτοκος, the mother of Chrift. Socrat. l. 7. c. 32. Concil. tom. 1. p. 1280. edit. Harduin. The defign of the council of Ephefus was, to fettle this notable difpute; or rather, to condemn Neftorius. When they met, Cyril of Alexandria, the avowed enemy of Neftorius, induced the bifhops prefent, of his own party, to proceed with great precipitance and violence to the condemnation of Neftorius, before the arrival of John bifhop of Antioch, and the bifhops who were with him; and that, in oppofition to the proteft of 60 or 70 bifhops, and of the emperor's commiffioner, whom they drove out of the affembly. Concil. tom. 1. p. 1351,—1354. And then they fent an account of what they had done, infcribed, " To Neftorius, a fecond Judas." Concil. tom. 1. p. 1434. When John and his party arrived, they depofed Cyril; Concil. tom. 1. p. 1450,—1455. and Cyril and his party, in return, depofed John; Concil. tom. 1. p. 1500. Evagr. l. 1. c. 5. p. 254, 255. And thus there fubfifted two councils, mutually condemning each other. To allay the ftorm,

had rather follow (next to the divine blessing on my own sincere enquiries) the judgment and guidance of some wise and good men, that I have known, than the publick the storm, the emperor gave his sanction to the deposition of Nestorius, Cyril, and Memnon an active partizan of Cyril's, (Concil. tom. 1. p. 1550. E. 1551. A, E. 1555. A.) and they were arrested by the emperor's commissioner, p. 1555,—1557. But he was afterwards brought (some say, by the money distributed amongst his courtiers by the deputies of Cyril, (p. 1580. C.) to alter his mind; to confirm, indeed, the deposition of Nestorius, whom he banished, (p 1670. A, B.); but to restore Cyril and Memnon. Ever since Cyril and his party have been esteemed the legitimate council of Ephesus. Isidorus of Pelusiota, in a letter to Cyril, treats him very justly as well as very freely, when he represents his conduct in this council to be that of a man pursuing only his own resentments, Epistol. l. 1. epist. 310. operum edit. Paris 1638.

The fourth general council of Chalcedon was occasioned by the extraordinary transactions of a second council of Ephesus, of which Dioscorus, bishop of Alexandria, was president; and in which the doctrine of the two natures in Christ after the incarnation was condemned, and the contrary doctrine of Eutyches affirmed. The menaces of the president, together with the soldiers and monks, who surrounded the council, terrified the whole assembly. Concil. tom. 2. p. 213. C, D. and Flavianus, bishop of Constantinople, who had condemned Eutyches, being accused by the president, and declared to be anathematized and deposed;

and

LETTER IV. 89

publick decisions of any or all the councils since the days of the apostles.

The third article which you exhibit a-
gainst

and appealing therefore from him, and some bishops at the same time interposing in his behalf; the president started up, and sternly called for the emperor's commissioners, by whose command the proconsul of Asia came in with the military, and a confused mob with chains and clubs and swords. Concil. tom. 2. p. 216. and some bishops not willing to declare, and others flying away, he cried out, " If " any one refuses to sign, with me he hath to contend," (tom. 2. p. 213. B.) and then he and another bishop carried about a blank paper, (Concil. tom. 2. p. 80. E. p. 94 D, E. p. 101. E. Evagr. l. 2. c. 4. p. 288.) and obliged them all to sign it. After which it was filled up with the charge of heresy against Flavianus, and the sentence of his deposition. Flavianus still excepting against the president, he and others fell furiously upon him, beating him barbarously, throwing him down, kicking and trampling upon him, insomuch that three days after he died of the bruises he had received in the council. Liberat. Breviar. c. 12. Niceph. Callist. l. 14. c. 47. tom. 2. p. 550. edit. Paris 1630.

The general council of Chalcedon, I say, was called upon occasion of the transactions and decisions of this second council of Ephesus; and after some struggle between the two contending parties, for and against Dioscorus; some crying out for the condemnation and banishment of the heretic,

gainst reviling the liturgy, is, that it involves in it " ingratitude, by denying in-
" dulgence and liberty of conscience to
" the members of the national church."

There
retic, for Christ had deposed him; and others, for his restoration to the council, to the churches; (Concil. tom. 2. p. 310. B.) the party against him prevailed, and he was deposed. (tom. 2. p. 377.) and the doctrine of the two natures, which had been condemned before, was now affirmed; the fathers crying out, " We believe as Pope Leo doth, " anathema to the dividers and confounders; we believe " as Cyril did; thus the orthodox believe, cursed be every " one who doth not believe so too." Concil. tom. 2. p. 305. E.

On this brief survey of these four general councils, will the reader believe, that they are by law joined with the scriptures, as judges of heresy, and as guides of that " *pu-* " *blick judgment*, which hath a better chance to be right " than the singular notions, or private judgment, of any " particular man?" Yet so it is.

It may, perhaps, by some persons, be esteemed an act of prudence to conceal the enormities of such famous assemblies of Christian bishops, lest the honour of Christianity should suffer by exposing them. But, I confess, I cannot be of this opinion. Christianity can never suffer, in the judgment of any impartial person, by the conduct of those turbulent and factious men, who have figured on the publick theatre in support of *political* religion; while it hath numberless advocates in every age, who, by their example as well as influence, promote the interest of *personal* religion; exhibiting the fairest

patterns

LETTER IV.

There would be little room, surely, Sir, to complain of violations of liberty of conscience, if, in contending for their respective dogmas, men never went beyond contemning and ridiculing one another: for, however censurable this may be, it certainly is not denying them liberty of conscience: that always implies restraint or

patterns of meekness, humility, contempt of the world, patience, contentment, purity and spirituality, universal benevolence and charity, as well as the most undissembled and fervent piety. Such men of sterling worth, such genuine Christians, who pass through the world, like a gentle current, which fertilizes the whole adjacent country, appear with no eclat in history; the good effects of their virtues being diffused in silence; while the restless and ambitious, who aim at wealth and power and pre-eminence, and bear down all before them, like resistless torrents, which desolate whole regions, attract observation for the changes they produce in the world, and the materials they furnish for the pen of the civil or ecclesiastical historian. Nevertheless, those good and righteous men, who have served their generation, in their particular stations, by their private virtues, will be hereafter had in everlasting remembrance; when those who have stood forth to the publick as the champions of tyranny or secular Christianity, will be covered with shame and everlasting contempt.

com-

compulsion, ideas very different from contempt and ridicule.

But perhaps, reviling the liturgy may be censured, as ungrateful, on account of the toleration indulged to Dissenters. It is not, however, to the church the Dissenters are peculiarly indebted for this blessing *. For though her governors promised them every mark of Christian temper and brotherly affection, when her fears of Popery ran high in the reign of James the Second; yet, as soon as the storm subsided, these promises were, in great measure, for-

---

* The author of the Alliance between the Church and State, in his Postscript in answer to Ld Bolingbroke, p. 2, 3 speaking both of the test-act and of the toleration, observes, that "this "reform of the English constitution happened not to be the "good work of the church, begun in the conviction of truth, "and carried on upon the principles of charity; but was "rather owing to the vigilance of the state, at one time, "vainly perhaps, anxious for the established religion, "(Char. II.) at another, wisely provident for the support "of civil liberty." (Will. III.) The author is certainly right with respect to the toleration: it was entirely the work of the state. King William engaged in it heartily; partly, no doubt, to strengthen the interest of civil liberty, of which

the

forgotten. It is to that great prince, King William, to whom the British constitution and liberties owe their preservation and security; and to those renowned patriots who first engaged, and then supported him, in the glorious enterprize; it is to these, and such as these, the Dissenters are, under God, alone obliged for their deliverance from unjust violence and oppression, and for being restored, in part, to their natural rights by the toleration. I say, to their natural rights: for religious liberty is one of those rights to which men are entitled by nature; as much so, as to their lives and properties; and it should be remembered, therefore, that the Dissenters

the Dissenters were to a man zealous friends; and partly, from a regard to religious liberty, of which he had all his life shewn himself a firm and steady patron. The test was not the work of Charles the Second: it was pushed on in opposition to the court by the patriots of those times, in order to secure the civil as well as the ecclesiastical constitution from the machinations of the Papists, by excluding them from publick offices; and the royal assent to it was procured by the Commons stopping the bill of supply till it was passed.

cannot

cannot be juſtly reckoned to be any more obliged to thoſe who *kindly* do not again deprive them of it, than they are to thoſe who, *as kindly*, do not ſeize on their eſtates, or take away their lives: an obligation which, I ſuppoſe, hath never been eſteemed a reaſon for any *peculiar gratitude*.

And now, Sir, notwithſtanding the exceptions which I have taken to your premiſes, I will leave you in full poſſeſſion of your concluſion: I will ſuppoſe, that the crime of reviling the liturgy is a complication of, "indecency, arrogance, and in- "gratitude:" and I will add, moreover, that it may poſſibly imply, (and, I think, it is the principal thing that can be implied in it, though you have not at all mentioned it), great malignity and inveteracy againſt the church. But, ſurely, to confiſcate a man's goods, and impriſon him for life, for any degree of any of theſe evil diſpoſitions towards the church, when diſcovered

LETTER IV.

covered only by words, (though it be frequently, and they be ever so open and explicit,) and not by any injurious and dangerous overt acts, must be confidered, one would think, by persons of humanity, and doubtless, therefore, by you, Sir, upon further reflection, to be somewhat *too severe and intolerant*. Notwithstanding all the bitterness with which the puritans inveighed against the offices of the church, (and which they did not do, till by oppression they were provoked almost to madness,) the passing this act, in my opinion, discovered a very intolerant spirit in those who, at that time, had the conduct of publick affairs.

But perhaps it may be said, that this measure was adopted only out of prudence, for the security of the national establishment. You inform us, that " the terror
" of these laws (for, you say, they seldom
" or never were fully executed) proved a
" principal means, under providence, of
" preserving

"preserving the purity as well as decency of our national worship *." Which, give me leave to say, Sir, is passing no great compliment upon the national worship.

But however that be: what had the church to fear from the revilings of the puritans, that she must fence herself around with human terrors? We are to suppose, she had all the truth and argument, as well as the encouragement of the civil magistrate, on her side. In this case, having recourse to human terrors was bringing disgrace on a good cause, and doing credit to a bad one. For the presumption, in most mens minds, is always in favour of the cause which is oppressed and persecuted; and that this is the case, is owing, partly to a certain generosity in mankind, which inclines them to side with the weakest, and those who are ill treated; and partly to a persuasion, which appears not

* Comment. vol. iv. p. 51.

wholly unreasonable, that while argument can be maintained, terror will not be employed. And for my own part, I am persuaded, that the church, instead of insuring its safety by these methods, greatly increased the number of its enemies, and inflamed their animosity and inveteracy. Had the governors of the church or state, at that time, made a few concessions, such as not only the puritans, but many wise and great men in the church, desired; or, in case they had not thought proper to do this, if they had indulged and tolerated those puritans, who could not in conscience conform, it is my opinion, the church would have been in no more danger from the puritans of that age, than it is now in from the Dissenters of this. Such severe laws occasioned the very crime they were intended to prevent; for they imbittered mens spirits, and inflamed their passions: and when the mind is greatly irritated, it is hardly in human nature to speak with temper and moderation, either of those by whom,

whom, or of that for which, men feel themselves ill-treated and oppressed.

I would further observe, (and it is an observation I would submit to the consideration of a gentleman of your profession, in particular) that, on supposition this act was levelled only, as you seem to imagine, against the bitter reproaches and insults of the puritans, it seems to have been drawn with too great a latitude of expression. I believe you will admit, and, I think, you have somewhere said something like it, that it is the excellence of any law to define offences and punishments with the utmost precision, that the subject may know distinctly what is lawful and what is forbidden. But is this the case with the act before us, supposing it to be designed merely against reviling and outraging the offices of the church? For, what is the precise idea of one who speaks, in open words, in derogation of the common prayer? Surely, under an expression of
such

LETTER IV.

such latitude may be included every man, who openly declares his disapprobation of any part of it; that is, every one who gives his reasons for not joining in the offices of the church; and he may, by a willing judge and jury, nay, ought, according to the literal sense of the words, to be convicted upon this statute. Now, supposing this law was intended only, as you seem to think, against insulting and reviling the liturgy; can so good a lawyer as Dr. Blackstone approve of a statute, which is so worded as to comprehend persons who are entirely innocent of the crime intended?

But in truth, I cannot help thinking, that it was the actual intention of those who promoted this act, to put an effectual stop, if possible, to the puritans *arguments* as well as their revilings; and that, on this account, the act was so expressed, as to include every man who finds fault with the common prayer, though only in a way of argument. For certainly, that is " in
" open

"open words speaking in derogation of it." The intent of the act at that time, I am afraid, was, to prevent the questioning any part of the service of the church, either in a way of reasoning or reviling.

Before Dr. Blackstone, therefore, had declared his approbation of this statute, and much more of the continuance of it to the present time, he should have considered, what persons and what cases, according to its literal and just construction, and perhaps according to its original intention, may be affected by it; and whether he would chuse to vindicate it in its full extent. In every view it appears to me very surprising, that you, Sir, who have expressed yourself, on various occasions, with so much liberality of sentiment, should think " the continuance of this act not too " severe and intolerant."

After such a declaration, I cannot be much surprised at your passing this encomium on the reign of Elizabeth, notwith-

LETTER IV.

withstanding it produced such severe laws against nonconformity, that " the refor-
" mation was then finally established with
" temper and decency, unsullied with par-
" ty-rancour, or personal caprice and re-
" sentment *." An impartial review of the ecclesiastical history of those times, as it is exhibited by Fuller, Strype, and other credible historians of the church of England, is, I think, sufficient to convince us, that there was, in that reign, a great deal of ill temper, party-rancour, and personal picque and resentment in the governors of the church, which entered much more than it should have done into their deliberations and conduct concerning ecclesiastical affairs. The Queen, it is true, at the entrance of her reign, discovered great policy and caution, in the measures she employed to take down the fabrick of Popery, which her sister Queen Mary had re-edified. Nevertheless, through the

* Comment. vol. iv. p. 48.

whole course of it, there were few demonstrations of temper and moderation in her, or in those governors of the church whom she principally esteemed and preferred; whereas there were many proofs and examples of unjust and cruel severity, towards those Protestants who disliked the least article in her ecclesiastical settlement, or who expressed, though in ever so humble and modest a manner, their desire of a further reformation. The truth is, she had entertained such lofty conceptions of her spiritual as well as temporal prerogative, and was disposed to maintain it, upon all occasions, with such rigour, as cannot be easily reconciled with any just notions of religious liberty, or with any regard to the sacred and inviolable rights of conscience.— I am, Sir, &c.

LETTER V.

SIR,

THE attempts to procure a further reformation in the church have been many and various. But while I enjoy my liberty as a Chriſtian, and a Proteſtant Diſſenter, I am not ſolicitous, on my own account, whether any alterations are made in the conſtitution or liturgy of the church of England. I deſpair of ever ſeeing the terms of conformity ſo enlarged and liberal, as to invite me into the eſtabliſhment. But when I conſider, that there are perſons already in the communion, and even in the orders of the church, who deſire, and endeavour to obtain, a reformation of various particulars which they, as well as

Protestant Dissenters, think ought to be reformed; I am sorry, on their account, and for the interest of religion in general, whenever I see difficulties thrown in the way of a design so laudable, and so desirable. In this view, it was with no small concern, that I observed you laying so much stress on the following sentiment: That " an alte-
" ration in the constitution or liturgy of
" the church of England, would be an in-
" fringement of the fundamental and es-
" sential conditions of the union between
" England and Scotland, and would great-
" ly endanger that union *."

I will first make some remarks upon this question, according to your state of it; and then explain the particular view in which, I think, it ought to be considered.

I observe that you allow, that, notwithstanding the act of union, and the conditions therein enacted, there is " a compe-

---

* Comment. vol. i. p. 98.

tent

" tent authority in the British parliament
" for making such alterations in the
" church *." And if so, whether the parliament should venture to exercise that power, is merely a question of prudence and expedience. You declare your opinion, that " it will endanger the union."
With submission, I cannot conceive, there could be any great danger in a parliamentary review and alteration of such things as it would be agreeable to the members of the church of England themselves should be altered; and especially if it be apparent to the whole world, that the design takes its rise in the church of England itself. The Scots would then have no reason to be alarmed; and I hardly think they would be so; because the case here supposed, is no precedent for any alterations in their church, except what they themselves shall desire. Could we suppose, indeed, an attempt made of alterations in the church of England, at a time when the Scots had

* See also Reply to Dr. Priestley, p. 20, 24.

reason

reason to apprehend a design, formed in England, to make alterations in the church of Scotland; and that alterations here were only made to furnish a kind of precedent for carrying that design into execution; they might, and probably would, be alarmed. But I cannot see, for my part, any dangerous consequences in the parliament's making what are generally considered to be real improvements (even tho' it should not be thought absolutely necessary to make them*) in either church, provided it be done only in conformity with the general sentiments and desire of the respective churches themselves. We see, in fact, that the passing the patronage-act, in respect to the church of Scotland, was attended with no such formidable conse-

---

* See Comment. vol. iv. p. 51. where the author saith, " It would now" (since the union) " be extremely unadvisable to make any alterations in the service of the church; unless it could be shewn, that some manifest impiety or shocking absurdity would follow from continuing it in its present form."

quences as you feem to apprehend; though it was an infringement of the union, the more dangerous, becaufe that act was paffed under the influence of Queen Anne's laft miniftry, in oppofition to the general fentiments of the Scottifh nation.

In what I have faid, I have left all confideration of the intention of the act of fecurity of the church of England, included in the act of union between the two nations, entirely out of the queftion. But after all, permit me to afk, Whether it was not the fpirit and defign of thefe acts of fecurity in both churches, to prevent the incroachments of one upon the other, after the union took effect? It muft certainly be admitted, that an apprehenfion of fuch incroachments upon each other, was the *occafion* of thofe acts; for if it had not been for the dangers apprehended by each church from the other, thofe acts of fecurity of the two churches had never been paffed at all: and from the *occafion* we may infer the *defign*.

Befides,

Besides, if no alteration must be made in either of the two churches, because the act of union hath settled things immutably in each; then the act of union amounts to a declaration of the legislature, that they would, and their posterity should, always think and act exactly as they did at that time: which, as Dr. Priestley observes, in his letter to you, published in the St. James's Chronicle of October 10. 1769, is so absurd, that one would not willingly impute it to two such august assemblies as the parliaments of both kingdoms.

But there is another view in which this point may be considered, independently of any enquiry, what was the design of the two parliaments, or the two nations, at the time when the act of union was enacted; and which, I think, is the true one: and it is this:

I believe it will be admitted, that, in all *pacta conventa*, or union treaties, those conditions which are previously insisted upon

upon by either of the contracting parties in its own favour, and in which the interest of the other is not involved, though they are ratified in ever so solemn a manner, are nevertheless alterable, with the free consent of that party who is alone interested therein. This is perfectly consonant to reason, and to the nature of such solemn pactions. Indeed, no conditions can be made so unalterable, that they cannot be reversed in the case which is here supposed; that is, where the only party interested in the condition, and who insisted upon it for his own behoof, releases the obligation, and consents to have it altered. And if this principle be allowed, the propriety of the application of it to the present case will appear, if we consider, that the union between England and Scotland, though an incorporating union in many, was not so in all respects; and particularly that in their ecclesiastical capacities, or with regard to their respective churches, the two nations, who were the original contracting parties, still continue

separate

separate bodies: I say, the two nations were the original contracting parties; for this should be carefully observed, that, strictly speaking, the two parliaments were not the contracting parties, but the two nations; for whom, and on whose behoof, the parliaments were only agents, or plenipotentiaries, executing an express or implied trust. And if so, either of the two churches, or nations, may authorise an alteration of any condition stipulated merely in its own favour, and in which the other hath no interest; that is, the English or the Scottish nation or church, may recede from the condition demanded and enacted in its own favour, even though most solemnly declared to be immutable. And on this footing, I mean, on the free consent of the party interested therein, the parliament of Great Britain may make the alterations in question.

Indeed, you tell us, that, " without " dissolving the union, you do not see how " the sense of either nation could now be

" sepa-

LETTER V.

" separately taken;" (that is) " how the Scots Peers or Commoners could be prevented from voting either for or against the repeal of the acts of uniformity, in case it were moved in either house *." And I admit, that as the two parliaments are now sunk into the one parliament of Great Britain, the sense of the two nations cannot be separately taken in parliament. But if the sense of the two churches, or, nations, in their separate ecclesiastical capacity, may be known, that will be a sufficient foundation for the parliament to proceed upon. For instance, if any alterations were requested of the parliament by the generality of either of the two churches or nations; or if, upon a motion in parliament for such alterations, and such motion being sufficiently known, they were not in a reasonable time petitioned against by any considerable number, the parliament might presume a general consent,

* Reply to Dr. Priestley, p. 17.

and must form their judgment of this from the notoriety of the fact.

And this is the footing upon which, I think, the case should be put; and not merely upon a competent authority in the British parliament to make alterations in the two churches. And I am of this opinion, because the parliament of Great Britain is to be considered as *guardian,* or *in trust,* for both churches; and therefore cannot have any *authority,* that is, *right,* inherent in itself (for *nemo potest, quod non jure potest*) to dispense with the conditions of the union, which were previously declared to be unalterable, *in those particular respects in which the two nations still continue separate bodies*; here, I think, nothing but the consent, expressed or implied, of each of these bodies, as to the condition stipulated in its own favour, can be sufficient warrant for an alteration.

Let this be illustrated by the case of the dissidents in Poland: Can it be thought, that there was an authority in the Polish diet

LETTER V.

diet to vacate the solemn *pacta conventa*, and the rights and privileges of the dissidents grounded upon them? I apprehend, the dissidents disallow, and protest against, such right or authority in the diet; and, I think, with reason; but they would have no such reason to complain of any infraction of the original settlement, if no alterations had been made but at their own request, or with their own free consent.

On the whole, this state of the question appears to me to be the only one that is consistent with the general nature of government as a trust *, with the sacred regard

---

* Nothing is more certain, than that government, in the general nature of it, is a trust in behalf of the people. And there cannot be a maxim, in my opinion, more ill-grounded, than that there must be an *absolute* or *arbitrary power* lodged somewhere in every government. If this were true, the different kinds of government in the world would be more alike, and upon a level, than they are generally supposed to be. In our own government in particular, though no one thinks with more respect of the powers, which the constitution hath vested in every branch of the legislature; yet I must be excused in saying, what is strictly true, that the whole legislature is so far from having an *absolute power*, that it hath not *any power*, in several cases that might

gard due to such *pacta conventa* as the act of union, and with the rights thereby reserved to each of the two churches; and, on those accounts, to be much preferable to acknowledging, on the one hand, a power in the parliament to dispense with such solemn conditions, when, and as far as, *they* shall think there is sufficient ground for it; or to holding, on the other hand, such conditions to be unalterable, whatever change of circumstances may render an alteration, in the general opinion, expedient and necessary.

might be mentioned. For instance, their authority does not extend to making the house of Commons perpetual, or giving that house a power to fill up their own vacancies; the house of Commons being the representatives of all the Commons of England, and in that capacity only a branch of the legislature; and if they concur in destroying the foundation on which they themselves stand; if they annihilate the rights of their constituents, and claim a share in the legislature upon any other footing, than that upon which the constitution hath given it to them; they subvert the very trust under which alone they act, and thereby forfeit all their authority. In short, they cannot dispense with any of those essential rights of the people, respecting their liberties, properties, or lives, the preservation of which ought to be the great object of government in general, as it is of our constitution in particular.

In

LETTER V.

In short, this argument, drawn from the immutability of the church in consequence of the act of union between the two nations, seems to me to be an useful engine to be played off by those who are averse to any alterations; but, I believe, (I speak only in general), would not have much stress laid upon it by those who are inclined to them.

However, if it be so, that the act of union renders every tittle and iota of the church constitution and liturgy immutable, this consideration furnishes the strongest argument for *their* separating entirely from the church, who are dissatisfied with the present state of things in it; inasmuch as this invariable settlement precludes all hope of future amendment.

In your answer to Dr. Priestley you say, you "have neither leisure, inclination, nor " ability to dip yourself in theological con- " troversy*." Will you suffer me to remind

* Reply to Dr. Priestley, p. 4.

you, Sir, that, if this be the case, you should not have *decided* a theological controversy, on which volumes have been written, in so summary a manner as you have done, when you say, " That many " Dissenters divide from the church upon " matters of indifference, or in other " words, upon no reason at all *."

To judge of the propriety and truth of this assertion, I first observe, that it is not agreed on both sides, that the things in question are indifferent. And, I think, whoever reads the Dissenting Gentleman's letters to Mr. White, and considers his objections to the present terms of conformity, must at least admit, that a great deal may be advanced to prove, that the things in debate are not indifferent, but such as very judicious as well as conscientious persons may reasonably scruple to comply with. However, even supposing them to be indifferent, I observe,

* Comment. vol. iv. p. 52.

That the authority, by which they are injoined and made neceſſary to the inſtitutions of Chriſt, and to a participation of Chriſtian ordinances, may be reaſonably called in queſtion. The twentieth article of the church of England aſſerts, indeed, "that the church hath power to decree rites and ceremonies, and hath authority in matters of faith." But this the Diſſenters muſt be allowed to controvert. They aſſert, that Chriſt alone hath this authority; that no power can make that neceſſary, which he hath not made neceſſary; and that what is indifferent in its own *nature*, ought to be left indifferent in *practice*, and ſhould not be bound upon Chriſt's ſubjects either by civil or ecclefiaſtical laws; neither of which can, in this caſe, be of any validity, as being both alike of human origin.

That "all things ſhould be done decently and in order *," they admit; and

* 1 Cor. xiv. 40.

in the sense of the apostle Paul, they assert with as much zeal as any other persons. But they think, there is a manifest difference between circumstances of natural decency and order, which are necessary to be agreed upon and observed, in order to the performance of any divine worship at all; and such rites and ceremonies, such additions to divine institutions, as are not at all necessary, in the reason of the thing, or by any law of Christ; but only injoined by a human, that is, in this case, incompetent authority. "A power in the church "to decree rites and ceremonies, and au- "thority in matters of faith," is a principle so extensive in its influence, that, under the shadow of it, have grown up all the enormous innovations and superstitions of the church of Rome*: And if Dissenters

---

* The following observations of Dr. Priestley, upon this head, in his View of the principles and conduct of the Protestant Dissenters, p. 59. are very sensible. "It should "be considered," saith he, "that a *power of decreeing* "*rites and ceremonies*, is a power absolutely indefinite, and "of

LETTER V.

ters should discover any aversion to giving countenance to such a principle, and its genuine consequences, excuse me, Sir, if I think, they are more than pardonable in

"of the very same kind with those claims, which, in
"things of a civil nature, always give the greatest alarm.
"A tax of a penny is a trifle; but a power of imposing
"that tax is never considered as a trifle, because it may im-
"ply absolute servitude in all who submit to it. In like
"manner, the enjoining of the posture of kneeling at the
"Lord's Supper is not a thing worth disputing about in
"itself, but the authority of enjoining it *is*; because it is,
"in fact, a power of making the Christian religion as bur-
"densome as the Jewish, and a power that hath actually
"been carried to that length in the church of Rome. Nor
"do we see any consistence in the church of England re-
"jecting the authority of Rome in these things, and impo-
"sing her own upon us."—

Again, p. 66. "Our ancestors, the old puritans, had
"the same merit in opposing the imposition of the surplice,
"that Hampden had in opposing the levying of ship-mo-
"ney. In neither case was it the thing itself they objected
"to, so much as the authority that enjoined it, and the
"danger of the precedent. And it appears to us, that the
"man who is as tenacious of his *religious* as he is of his
"*civil liberty*, will oppose them both with equal firmness.

"All the difference, then, in the conduct of men who
"equally value their liberty, will be in the *time* and *manner*
"of opposing these incroachments upon it. The man of a
"strong and enlarged mind will always oppose these things

"in

in so doing, and should not have been represented as acting upon no reason at all.— I am, Sir, &c.

" in the beginning, when only the resistance can have any
" effect; but the weak, the timid, and short-sighted, will
" attempt nothing till the chains are rivetted, and resist-
" ance is too late. In civil matters, the former will make
" his stand at the levying of the first penny by *improper autho-*
" *rity*; and in matters of religion, at the first, though the
" most trifling ceremony, that is, without reason, made
" necessary; whereas the latter will wait till the load, in
" both cases, is become too heavy to be either supported
" or thrown off." And by these reasons he supports his remark, p. 58. that " the opposition made by the first
" nonconformists to the injunction of a few ceremonies,
" was an argument of great *strength of mind*; and that they
" acted upon more just and enlarged views of things, than
" those who superciliously affect to stigmatize them as men
" of *weak minds.*" Whether the puritans understood the principles of liberty so thoroughly, and acted upon such enlarged views of things, as they are here represented to have done, I will not pretend to say. Of this, however, I am very certain, that all these observations are true and just as applied to the modern Dissenters.

LETTER VI.

SIR,

I Obferve in your Commentaries a very remarkable paffage, which afferts the abfolute neceffity of excluding all Diffenters from civil offices, as a thing *effential* to the *very idea* of a national eftablifhment. —You fay, " He," (that is, the magiftrate) " is bound to protect the eftablifh-
" ed church, by admitting none but its ge-
" nuine members to offices of truft and e-
" molument: for if every fect was to be
" indulged in a free communion of civil
" employments, the idea of a national e-
" ftablifhment would at once be deftroy-
" ed, and the Epifcopal church would be
" no

"no longer the church of England*." That is extraordinary indeed! Some have talked of the security which may arise to the church from this exclusive privilege; and you intimate it yourself, when you say, it is the magistrate's duty to *protect* the church by this method. Others have insisted upon I know not what kind of alliance or contract, in which this exclusive privilege was stipulated for the church. But that the church would lose her *existence* and *essence* without it, seems to be very strange. What! cannot the church be established in the possession and enjoyment of her own peculiar temporalities; her tythes, prebends, canonries, archdeaconries, deanries, and bishopricks by law, unless she engross all civil as well as ecclesiastical offices to herself? Can there be no legal establishment of, and no legal and national provision made for, a *church*, unless all the offices and emoluments of the *state* are annexed to it? Was there no

* Comment. vol. iv. p. 53.

national

national church properly established by law in England till the test-act was enacted, which appropriated all civil offices to persons of her communion, in the reign of Charles the Second? and is there none now in Scotland, where civil offices are not confined to the Presbyterians, who have been hitherto supposed to be the ecclesiastical establishment in that country? Is there, I say, no such establishment in Scotland? is the very idea of it destroyed, and the Presbyterian church no longer the established church of that part of the united kingdom? I apprehend, this will hardly be affirmed; and if so, an exclusive right to civil offices cannot be essential to the very idea of a church-establishment.

Indeed, I would not willingly suppose any thing so unjust can be essential to an ecclesiastical establishment. For certainly good subjects, if they are by law deprived of the capacity of serving their king and country, in those offices for which they are

are qualified, and which possibly they might otherwise obtain, are injured by such exclusion. I do not say, that the actual possession of civil offices is the right of any subject; but a capacity of being elected or appointed to them, is the right of every good subject; and being deprived of that capacity is plainly an injury; and every injury done a man merely for his religion, and not on a civil account, is, in my opinion, a degree of persecution: I know no other definition of persecution, than that it is an injury inflicted on a person for his religious principles or profession only.

A test-law, appropriating all civil offices to the members of the church, hath been vindicated, even on supposition of its being contrary to the law of nature, by instances of municipal laws, made, in direct opposition to the law of nature, for the publick good[*]. But in such cases, the advantage

---

[*] See the Bishop of Gloucester's Alliance between Church and State, p. 320. edit. 4.

to the publick ought to be very apparent, and of confiderable moment; and even then, is rather to be confidered as an *excufe* for fuch deviations from the law of nature, or general principles of equity, in the prefent imperfect ftate of fociety, than as a full and abfolute *juftification* of them. However, fhould an exclufion of good fubjects from civil offices on a religious account appear, upon examination, not to be at all for the publick good, then the very foundation of this defence (fuch as it is) of an exclufive teft is entirely deftroyed. The queftion therefore is, What is that publick good arifing from a teft-law, and the exclufion of good fubjects from civil offices, which overbalances the right that every fuch fubject hath, on principles of reafon and equity, to a capacity of being appointed to fuch offices?

Upon the moft general view of this point, it cannot appear to be for the good of the *magiftrate*, or the *ftate*, to be deprived of the power of availing itfelf of
the

the services of any good subjects. It is, surely, for the advantage of the state, that none should be rendered incapable of civil employments, but those whose affections or principles render them suspected to the civil government; that is, who do not give proper testimony of their being good subjects: for the more numerous the persons are who are capable of such appointments, the greater is the probability of a proper choice, provided those who make it discharge their duty to the publick with fidelity and judgment.

It may be alledged, perhaps, that the magistrate hath wisely consented to grant the church this exclusive privilege, in order to obtain the *greater good* of the special services of the church, in inforcing the duties of imperfect obligation, such as gratitude, hospitality, generosity, &c. which human laws cannot effectually inforce; and of an alliance with her, and a right by grant from the church to a supremacy over her,

her, and to the power of appointing her ministers and officers.

With regard to the service which the church does the state, by inforcing the duties of imperfect obligation, and by which she is supposed to merit, in part, her exclusive privilege to civil offices; I observe, that if this be a reason for allowing capacity of civil employments to good subjects of any one religious persuasion, it is a valid reason for extending it to good subjects of all religious persuasions; and in particular, to the Protestant Dissenters. For, in their religious assemblies, these virtues are inculcated, perhaps with as good effect, and with as much utility to society, as amongst Christians of any other denomination. Upon this state of the case, therefore, no sufficient cause can be assigned, why they should be excluded from a reasonable and proportionable share of the favour of the state.

As for the church's giving up her independence and supremacy, and the appointment

ment of her officers or ministers, to the state; it may be proper to enquire, to what this condescension, on the part of the church, may be supposed to amount. And here it should be remarked, that the state hath a right to a supremacy over all persons, whether clergy or laity, of every religious persuasion, within her dominions; a right, founded in the nature of civil government, independent of any grant from the church; and in this sense, the church could confer upon the state no supremacy which it had not before; it could not give it any new subjects, or increase its civil power.

The meaning, therefore, of this grant of supremacy must be, that the church admitted the state to a supremacy in causes ecclesiastical, and to the appointment of her church-officers; in lieu of which she claims an exclusive right to the possession of civil offices. And these, it is said, are the terms of the grand alliance between the church and state, upon which is
grounded

grounded the equity of a teſt-law, excluding all from the poſſeſſion of civil offices, except the members of the eſtabliſhed church. But it doth not appear, that any ſuch terms were ever concerted and agreed between the church and the ſtate; it appears, on the contrary, that no ſuch *can be* ſuppoſed or *implied*, on any fair and equitable principles. For, all the peculiar temporalities of the church being ſolely the grant of the ſtate, and her particular form and conſtitution being eſtabliſhed by its laws, the government of the church of courſe belonged to that authority which formed and endowed it; and when the ſtate appoints the miniſters and officers of the church, ſhe doth it upon this footing, that the proviſion made for their ſupport is her donation and eſtabliſhment. Now, on this ground, the ſtate was in undiſputed poſſeſſion of all the power of church-government, and of the appointment of church-officers, which ſhe at preſent enjoys, before any teſt was appointed, or nonconformists were by law excluded from civil offices. This exclusive right, therefore, now claimed by the church, to the offices of the state, could be no part, no term, no condition of the supposed *original* treaty of alliance between the church and state. The claim is entirely *novel*; it is an usurpation upon the state, an attempt to introduce a new term or condition into the original contract, which ought therefore to be rejected as inadmissible.

If it be said, that the church hath purchased this exclusion of Protestant Dissenters from civil offices, by consenting to a toleration of their religious profession and worship; I observe, that this free enjoyment of their religious liberty was a natural right, of which they were never deprived but with manifest injustice; and the granting of their religious liberty, therefore, or the repairing of one act of injustice, can never be considered as a sufficient reason, or tolerable excuse, for a violation of their civil

civil rights; that is, committing another act of injustice.

If it be further alledged, that the church's exclusive enjoyment of civil offices comes in as a balance to the toleration, as an accession of strength to the church; in order to counterpoise the danger which might accrue to her, were Dissenters admitted to a free enjoyment of civil offices: * (whereas her security before the toleration

---

* Thus argues the author of The Alliance, &c. p. 296, 297. and gives himself the credit of being of the same sentiments with King William, whom he stiles, perhaps justly, the best and greatest of our monarchs; applauding his equal conduct in his different stations of Prince of Orange and King of England: which conduct he thus represents. " When King James, a *Papist*, demanded of his son-in-" law, with whom he was then on good terms, his appro-" bation of a *toleration* and *abolition of the test*, the Stathol-" der readily concurred with the scheme of a *toleration*, but " utterly condemned an *abolition of the test*. When after-" wards he became King of a free people, the *Protestant* " Dissenters, likewise, in their turn, demanded both. " His conduct was uniformly the same. He gave them a " *toleration*, but would not consent to *abolish the test*." The only fault I find with this account is, that it is not *history*, but *fable*. The fact is, that when King James asked the Prince's approbation of the abolition of the test, he meant,

tion confifted in this, that every man, whether in or out of office, was by law confidered as a member of the church, and indifpenfably obliged to conformity:) I fay,

and the Prince underftood him to mean, a repeal of it as to the *Papifts*, as well as the Proteftant Diffenters; and it was with refpect to the former the Prince refufed his approbation. When afterwards he became King of England, he was fo far from refufing the *Proteftant Diffenters* the repeal of the teft as to *them*, that he had the defign very much at heart; he fignified it in council, and, in a fpeech on the occafion, earneftly recommended it to his parliament, that, while he " doubted not they would fufficiently provide a-
" gainft Papifts," they would " leave room for the admif-
" fion of all Proteftants that were willing and able to ferve:" adding, " This conjunction in my fervice will tend to the
" better uniting you amongft yourfelves, and the ftrength-
" ening you againft your common adverfaries." And accordingly, when a claufe for repealing the teft as to Proteftant Diffenters, which was inferted in the bill for fettling the oaths, was rejected; the King, being refolved to purfue his defign, procured another claufe to be propofed to be inferted in the fame bill, in order to qualify all perfons for places, who, within a year before or after their admiffion into them, had received the facrament, either according to the ufage of the church of England, or *in any other Proteftant congregation:* which claufe was alfo rejected, notwithftanding the influence of the court in its favour. See Tindal's Continuation of Rapin, vol. 1. p. 120,—123. edit. 8vo. 1758. The conduct of the Prince and the King
was

LETTER VI.

say, should this be alledged, it will come under consideration, when we examine the nature of the *security* which the *church* derives from an exclusive test.

For,

was equal and consistent; but, as we have seen, totally different from the ideas of this author.

It should be observed, that the original design of the test was, not to exclude the Protestant Dissenters, but the Papists. It was brought in by the patriots in the reign of Charles the Second, under their apprehensions of Popery and a Popish successor; and when, during the debate in the House of Commons, it was observed, that it was drawn in such a manner as to comprehend the Protestant Dissenters, the court-party endeavoured to avail themselves of that circumstance in order to defeat the bill. But the dissenting members disappointed them, by declaring, that they had rather confide in the justice and generosity of parliament to pass some future bill in their favour, than be the occasion of retarding or defeating the security, which the present bill was calculated to afford to the liberties of their country. And this genuine patriotism produced soon afterwards a bill for their relief from the penal laws; but the parliament was prorogued, through the resentment of the court, to prevent its passing. And when, notwithstanding this, a bill in favour of the Dissenters did afterwards pass both houses, and lay ready for the royal assent, the court ventured upon a very extraordinary expedient: the clerk of the crown was ordered to convey away the bill; and, accordingly, it was never afterwards to be found. The continuance of the test act, therefore, to the present time, and

For, if this plea of publick good, as the basis of an exclusive test, does not relate to the good of the state, perhaps it may to the good of the church.

And the exclusion of Dissenters from all publick offices, is the reward they enjoy for their generous and disinterested patriotism.

Indeed, this particular test, receiving the sacrament according to the rites of the church of England, as it was designed, so it was calculated, to exclude the Papists, rather than the Protestant Dissenters; for the former, it was apprehended, would not comply with the established church in this office above all others; and to increase the difficulty on their part, they were expresly required, besides the oaths of allegiance and supremacy, to renounce transubstantiation: whereas it was, at that very time, no uncommon thing for Protestant Dissenters, to receive the sacrament occasionally in the church of England, in order to express their charity towards it as a part of the church of Christ. This was the case with Mr. Baxter, Dr. Bates, and others of their leading clergymen, as well as many of their laity. Indeed, after the test was enacted, many of these altogether abstained from this practice; because they would not act upon a suspicious motive, and because they totally disapproved the use of a religious ordinance as a civil test. But this consequence of appointing the sacrament as a test, was not likely to be foreseen at the time the act was enacted. And therefore, I think, we may on the whole infer with reason, that it was not particularly levelled against the Protestant Dissenters. If it had been the design of

LETTER VI.

And, doubtless, it is for *her good*, in one sense; namely, for her *emolument*, that her members only should enjoy civil offices. But, provided this claim does not appear to be *just* as well as profitable, it would be an ill compliment to the church to suppose her capable of continuing and maintaining it. And where, indeed, *is the equity* of her demanding, besides that ample provision which is made for her support by law, and to which the whole nation contributes, an exclusion of all, who are not in her communion, from the opportunity of serving their king and country, and enjoying the honours or emoluments of such services? Where is the equity, I say, that, instead of being satisfied, not merely with her own peculiar revenues, but with that share of civil offices and

of the legislature, to exclude all from civil offices but those who have a real affection for the constitution and worship of the church, they would doubtless have appointed the test to be, not merely once taking the sacrament at church, but a stated and constant conformity to all its religious services.

emoluments which would fall to the members of her communion, and which undoubtedly would be by far the largest and most considerable, she must possess an exclusive right to the whole? and where, in reason and justice, is her title to such a monopoly? The "kingdom of Christ is "not of this world;" and religion, much less any peculiar form of it, can be no foundation for a claim to all civil offices and emoluments in any country; because *dominion is not founded in grace*, nor are the *saints of any communion*, as such, entitled to all those good things, which those who are possessed of dominion have to bestow.

These are principles so just and indisputable, that some of the warmest friends of establishments and exclusive tests have been forced to confess, that they are, neither of them, founded in *truth*, but in *utility:* that when a particular religion is established by law, and fenced with the sole and exclusive privilege of enjoying civil offices and emoluments; this is not done on account

count of its being the *true religion*, but the *religion of the majority*; which, as such, is taken into alliance by the state, and so established and privileged for the publick good. Provided, therefore, it can be shewn, that this goodly fabrick no way contributes to publick utility, it cannot any longer be supported, but must fall to the ground.

As for the supposition, that it conduces to the utility of the *state*, that I have already considered. As for the utility of the *church*, if by that be meant her profit or emolument, she should, as I before observed, insist upon no gain but that which is fair and honourable, none to the prejudice of other good subjects, where they have a just and equitable claim.

But if this publick utility is understood to refer to the *security* and *protection*, which is apprehended to be afforded to the church, by the exclusion of all others, except the members of her own communion, from civil offices; that is a point which remains now

now to be confidered: For you tell us, that " the magiftrate is bound to *protect* " the eftablifhed church, by admitting " none but its genuine members to offices " of truft and emolument."

The danger of the church, and the ftrength of that fecurity which is afforded by a teft-law, in cafe fhe be in danger, hath, I think, been greatly magnified. Indeed, her danger feems to be a mere chimera. I am perfuaded, the church would be in no danger from the Proteftant Diffenters, who have very little difpofition to moleft her; and would have lefs ftill, if fhe left them in full poffeffion of their civil rights. The removal of any odious mark of diftinction, and ground of jealoufy and envy, as it leaves men more at eafe, fo in greater good humour with themfelves and others, and very little difpofed to quarrel about modes of faith and modes of worfhip. That is not, indeed, at all the temper of the prefent age; nor is it likely to be fo of their pofterity, unlefs the fpirit
of

of persecution should arise in the church or state. That would set in motion a certain spring and elasticity there is in human nature, which rises against oppression. But in quiet and peaceable times, when principles of moderation and liberty universally prevail, this elastic spring is wholly relaxed. And the more liberal and equitable, therefore, the temper and conduct of the church and state are, towards men of different religious persuasions, who are good subjects, the less danger is there of molestation to either. An equitable disposition in the church, to permit all without exception to enjoy, in their full extent, their natural rights, would be a much greater security to her, than any exclusive or even penal laws. For, the principles of impartial liberty form the prevailing character of the present age, and are, in a manner, universal amongst the Protestant Dissenters. Liberty, religious liberty especially, is their idol; in their attachment to which, for the most part, they
are

are more tenacious, than they are in their affection to any peculiar distinguishing tenets, which divide them from the church, or from one another. And this liberty they would no more violate in others, than be easy to see it violated in themselves *.

But

---

* Dr. Burton, (in his Commentariolus Thomæ Secker Archiep. Cantuar. memoriæ sacer) speaking of the opposition which hath been made to the scheme of establishing bishops in America, exclaims, " Iniqui homines & maligni ! " qui libertatis, quam ipsi sibi arrogant effrænatam, jus aliis " à se dissidentibus concedi nolunt !" I am not certain whether these words refer to the American Presbyterians and Independen's, or to the English Dissenters. Perhaps the Doctor would have no great objection to our understanding them both of the Americans and the Dissenters; for he does not seem to have much complaisance for either. However that be, I may venture to say of both, that so far from showing themselves, by their opposition to this scheme, to be the enemies, I apprehend, they have shown themselves to be the friends, of liberty. When they are convinced, that the scheme of sending bishops to America hath not the advancement of ecclesiastical power in view, and will not be prejudicial to the liberty of Christians of other persuasions; when the plan shall appear to be solely this, not only that the bishops shall be invested with the mere powers of confirmation and ordination, and of regulating their own clergy, but shall be excluded, by express act of parliament, or by provincial acts previously passed, and solemnly ratified

LETTER VI.

But if any could be found, who were disposed to give the church molestation, while she hath so vast a majority in the kingdom, and especially in both Houses of Parliament, (and I cannot see, that the repeal of the test would make any alteration in

fied by act of parliament, (in some such manner as the acts of security of the two churches, in the union between England and Scotland,) from enjoying the least degree of temporal power; (always supposing, that the salaries for their support shall be drawn only from those who profess to be of the Episcopal persuasion;) then, I apprehend, if I may judge of the Americans by what I have heard of them, and of the Dissenters by those with whom I am acquainted, they will be so far from opposing, that they will be advocates for such a scheme. And in so doing they will allow others the very same liberty which they claim themselves. For, though they are friends to liberty, they are enemies to temporal power in the hands of ecclesiastics, presbyters as well as bishops. Some things have dropped from the Archbishop, in his letter to Mr. Walpole, which give ground to surmise, that the whole of what is intended, is not so mild and moderate as his panegyrist supposes. " The proposal " is," saith the Archbishop, " that the bishops shall exercise " such jurisdiction over the clergy of the church of England " in those parts, as the late bishop of London's commissa- " ries did, or *such as it might be thought proper that any fu-* " *ture commissaries should,*" (and who knows what that may be?) " if this design were not to take place," p. 2. And

in this respect,) the apprehension of danger from the Dissenters being admitted to such offices, as a few amongst them may be qualified for, and likely to obtain, must be entirely groundless. It is my firm opinion, that the repeal of the test would be a greater

to the question, " How any persons can undertake to pro-
" mise, that no additional powers shall hereafter be pro-
" posed and pressed on the colonies, when bishops have
" once been settled?" he answers, " that, strictly speak-
" ing, nothing of that nature can ever be promised in any
" case," p. 6, 7. And he saith, that " there seems no
" necessity, that the affair should ever come into parliament;
" for, as the law now stands, suffragan bishops may be or-
" dained with the King's approbation; and the bishop of
" London may send these, instead of presbyters, for his com-
" missaries," p. 21. If the American Presbyterians and Independents, and their friends the Dissenters in England, are more jealous than they need be of the scheme of sending bishops to America, it is owing to the evident reluctance there is in the most moderate patrons of this scheme, to the Episcopal power being laid under any positive restraint or limitation, and to their expressing a desire of having that matter left entirely open; as well as to the conduct of the society for propagating the gospel, who expend a great disproportion of their revenues in countries where Christianity is already in a flourishing condition, merely to proselyte the inhabitants to Episcopacy; and whose missionaries are, many of them, of the old *jure divino* stamp, who think Episcopacy

a greater disadvantage to the body of Dissenters, than to the established church; that it would rather diminish than increase their numbers. For, in general, men are not much inclined to shock all the principles on which they have acted; and desert a party with which they are connected, at once, on a lucrative motive; but they may be gradually softened and relaxed

copacy and the uninterrupted succession essential to the validity of religious ordinances, and to the Christian as well as the ministerial character. It is very unhappy, if the society, as the Archbishop intimates, p. 4. can procure " few to go " from hence, in the character of missionaries, but persons " of desperate fortunes, low qualifications, and bad or " doubtful characters;—a great part of whom," saith he, " are Scotch; and I need not say," he adds, " what " chance there is, that Episcopal clergymen of that coun- " try may be disaffected to the government." In this state of things, the Americans, those especially who are not of the Episcopal persuasion, may reasonably expect some barrier, some security, supposing bishops sent to America with spiritual characters only, against their assuming, or possessing afterwards, any degree of temporal authority. And unless this be done, the opposition of them and their friends here, to such a design, is no proof that they are enemies to the liberties of others, but only that they are willing to preserve their own.

in

in their principles, by the new connections into which the poffeffion of publick offices would introduce them, by the influence of general cuftom, and of what is efteemed polite and fafhionable, and by the example of their fuperiors, or of the majority; provided they are not difgufted and revolted by any ungenerous compulfion or reftraint. In fuch circumftances, no confiderable numbers, if any, would be found mad enough to embark in the dangerous enterprize of overturning an eftablifhment, fo well guarded and fenced by law, as that of the church of England, and to which the nation hath been fo long accuftomed. And provided, in any future time, fhe fhould be improved in her conftitution, in her publick forms, and in the terms of conformity to her lay and minifterial communion, there would be no human profpect, fcarcely a poffibility, of fhaking her foundations, fhould any be inclined to attempt it. For, the broader the bafis on which fhe ftands, fhe ftands the firmer. And there-

LETTER VI. 145

therefore, comprehensive, not exclusive measures should, in all prudence, be adopted and pursued by those who would approve themselves her truest and best as well as warmest friends.

If, to all these considerations, you should oppose the destruction of the ecclesiastical constitution, in the last century, by the sectaries: I beg leave to observe, that the true cause, and at bottom the only cause, of the overthrow of the church at that time, was, that her leading men and governors had been, in some cases the authors, and in others the instruments, of civil as well as ecclesiastical tyranny. Their oppressions and persecutions had been deeply felt by the puritans, who had some zeal for religion; and their slavish doctrines, and arbitrary measures, pernicious and fatal as they were to civil liberty, had given such a turn to mens minds in general, as enabled some religious zealots, in conjunction with the Scots, who insisted

L upon

upon the destruction of Episcopacy before they would move to the assistance of the parliament when their affairs were at a low ebb, to overturn the ecclesiastical constitution. But what is the inference from hence? that the permitting of the Dissenters to enjoy the common rights of good subjects, would endanger the church a second time? I think the reverse: that, as the tyranny of the church and state proved, by a strange concurrence of circumstances, the ruin of both; lenity, and some degree of the same magnanimity in this case, which, you say, was discovered in the toleration, would, in this instance as well as in the former, tend to her establishment and preservation. For, as we see in fact, that every instance of it, which hath been hitherto exercised, hath had that effect; we have reason to conclude, that every further instance of it would undoubtedly have the same.

Besides, what security can be derived to the

LETTER VI.

the church from a man's now and then receiving the sacrament in it, for the sake of a good place? That is, I own, a mark of *his affection for the place*; but very little, I am sure, of his affection for the church; to which he may, notwithstanding a compliance obtained by a bait so alluring, be still a false friend, or a determined enemy.

And, as there are these objections to a test in general, affecting Protestant Dissenters; so there are some, I think, no inconsiderable ones, to the particular nature of the test by law appointed; namely, that leading persons to take the sacrament with wrong views, who would not otherwise do it at all, and who have no proper notions of and right dispositions for it, it gives ground to consider it as an abuse of a sacred ordinance, which was appointed for the ends of religion only, to temporal and worldly views and purposes; and as a strong temptation to hypocrisy:

pocrisy: and though they are criminal who do not resist it; yet, neither are they innocent, who lay the snare in their way.

I am, Sir, &c.

LETTER VII.

SIR,

IT will be found, I believe, that the observations which I have occasionally made upon the character of the Protestant Dissenters are strictly just: that their principles are calculated to render them the firm and invariable friends of the civil constitution of their country. You observe, that " in all ages and countries *civil and eccle-* " *siastical tyranny* are mutually productive of " each other *." I think it must be equally true, that *religious* and *civil liberty* have a reciprocal influence in producing and supporting one another; and accordingly the

* Comment. vol. iv. p. 103.

Protestant Dissenters are at least as likely as any, to be warmly and steadily attached to both. I cannot forbear, therefore, taking notice, with surprize, of a passage in your chapter of *Præmunire*, which, notwithstanding I have endeavoured to put the most favourable construction upon it, I cannot reconcile to the supposition of your having any tolerable idea, what the principles are which generally prevail amongst the Protestant Dissenters. After a very extraordinary panegyrick upon the church of England, and the clergy of her persuasion *, of which I am not inclined, in the

---

* " It is the glory of the church of England," you say,
" as well as a strong presumptive argument in favour of
" the purity of her faith, that she hath been (as her prelates
" on a trying occasion once expressed it: Address to Jam. II.
" 1687.) in her principles and practice ever most unque-
" stionably loyal. The clergy of her persuasion, holy in
" their doctrines, and unblemished in their lives and con-
" versation, are also moderate in their ambition, and en-
" tertain just notions of the ties of society and the rights
" of civil government, As in matters of faith and mora-
" lity they acknowledge *no guide but the scriptures*, so, in
" matters of external polity and of private right, they de-
" rive

LETTER VII.

the least, to dispute the propriety, you give us a striking contrast in these remarkable words: " Whereas the principles of
" those who differ from them, as well in
" one extreme as the other, are equally
" and totally destructive of those ties and
" obligations by which all society is kept
" together; equally incroaching on those
" rights, which reason, and the original
" contract of every free state in the uni-
" verse, have vested in the sovereign

" rive all their title from the civil magistrate; they look
" up to the King as their head, to the parliament as their
" lawgiver, and pride themselves in nothing so justly, as
" in being true members of the church emphatically *by*
" *law* established. Whereas the principles of those who
" differ," &c. It cannot be doubted, that a clergy so holy and moderate and unambitious, and so warmly attached to the SCRIPTURES *as their* ONLY *guide in matters of faith and morality*, and to the civil magistrate in respect to matters of external polity, will do their utmost to procure a reform of various particulars in their ecclesiastical constitution, discipline, and worship; and especially a repeal of the twentieth article, by which the CHURCH is said to have *power to decree rites and ceremonies*, and *authority in matters of faith*; and likewise of the law, by which the *four first general councils*, in *conjunction* with the scriptures, are made judges of heresy.

" power;

" power; and equally aiming at a diſtinct
" independent ſupremacy of their own,
" where ſpiritual men and ſpiritual cauſes
" are concerned *."

Popiſh principles, undoubtedly, are one extreme to which you here allude; and, I think, diſſenting principles, at leaſt when they are carried to their utmoſt length, muſt be the other. It is true, the examples, which you immediately produce in ſupport of this branch of your aſſertion, are of ſome enthuſiaſts both at home and abroad in the laſt century: " The dread-
" ful effects," you ſay, " of ſuch a reli-
" gious bigotry, when actuated by erro-
" neous principles even of the Proteſtant
" kind, are ſufficiently evident from the
" hiſtory of the Anabaptiſts in Germany,
" the Covenanters in Scotland, and that
" deluge of ſectaries in England, who
" murdered their ſovereign, overturned
" the church and monarchy, ſhook every

* Comment. vol. iv. p. 103.

" pillar

"pillar of law, juftice, and private property, and moft devoutly eftablifhed a kingdom of the faints in their ftead."

The only objection I think proper to make to the fentiment fuggefted in this round and warm paragraph, is, that it cannot vindicate the univerfality of your cenfure on the principles of thofe who, among Proteftants, differ from the church; unlefs upon fuppofition, that the principles of all Proteftant Diffenters are of the fame nature and tendency with thofe, which, being carried to an extreme by the Anabaptifts in Germany, and the Fifth-monarchy-men in England, in the laft century, produced very extravagant confequences. This conftruction offers itfelf fo readily, that, if it was not your intention to ftigmatize the Diffenters of the prefent age in any degree, but only fome particular enthufiafts of the laft age both at home and abroad, it might furely have been expected, that fome exceptive or qualifying expreffions fhould have been inferted in their

their favour. And after what you have said of the modern Dissenters, in your Reply to Dr. Priestley, I hope this will be done in future editions.

In the mean time, as I apprehend this paragraph will be understood to intimate, that the Dissenters hold principles unfriendly to society, and to civil government; principles which, in the extreme, have produced the most fatal effects, both at home and abroad; in justice to them, (though not in opposition to you, if you really do not intend this censure for them,) I shall offer a few remarks, in order to show, that the principles of the Dissenters are entirely the reverse both of Popish principles, and of those enthusiastic principles which you mention, and can never produce the dreadful consequences to civil government which flow from either.

The church of Rome, indeed, asserts her own supremacy over the civil power,

LETTER VII.

in every country*. And accordingly she demands an absolute submission in all her members, subversive not only of the rights of a free people, but of all the obligations of society, and the very foundations of civil polity. She claims an utter exemption of

---

* This claim the church of Rome hath always advanced, and, where-ever she hath had opportunity, exercised, without ever in a single instance giving it up. Since the Reformation, the times have been daily growing more unfavourable to the exercise of that enormous power, which formerly held the civil authority all over Europe in absolute subjection and dependence. But the church, ever attentive to her favourite supremacy, still takes every method to prevent its further depression, and even to restore it, if possible, to its former glorious exaltation. With this worthy design, a large folio volume, in Latin, in a small type, was printed in England (without any name of place or printer) in the year 1753, (of which I have a copy now in my hands,) under the care of the Jesuits, and the impression sent to Portugal, for the use of the ecclesiasticks in that kingdom. It is intitled, Opusculum-Theologico-Juridicum, de utroque Recursu: in Judicem, scilicet, competentem et incompetentem : quinque libris distinctum : in quibus agitur, in lib. 1. De Recursu ad Judicem competentem, puta ab Ecclesiastico ad Ecclesiasticum, de sæculari ad sæcularem, vel *ad Ecclesiasticum Superiorem :* in 2do vero, De eodem ad Judicem INCOMPETENTEM ; puta, ab Ecclesiastico ad Sæcularia Tribunalia, &c. So that,

of all ecclesiastical persons, and of all their rights and possessions, from the jurisdiction and authority of the magistrate. But is there the least similarity to this, in the sentiments of the Protestant Dissenters? No, certainly. It is their opinion, I own, that

that, according to the doctrine which this book is intended to establish, by an infinite number of reasons and authorities (such as they are) from the decrees of Popes, of councils, of the holy office of Inquisition, and of numberless Romish canonists and casuists, the *civil* power hath NEVER any controul over the *ecclesiastical*, but the *ecclesiastical* ALWAYS over the *civil*. And even the power, assumed and exercised by the Popes in the darkest ages, of deposing emperors, kings, and all other princes and magistrates, is explicitly asserted and maintained. This work, so much adapted to promote the glory of holy church, is published under the patronage of the King of Kings; Sub *Regis Regum* patrocinio, omnibus Regibus, Principibus, ac Judicibus, tum Ecclesiasticis, tum Sæcularibus, dicatum. The author the Bishop of *Algarve:* Autore Excellentissimo ac Reverendissimo D. Ignatio à S. Teresia Portucalensi, Excanonico Regulari S. Augustini Congregationis S. Crucis Collimbriensis, Archiepiscopo Goano, Primate Orientis, Indiani Status semel, et iterum, Sæcuiari Ex gubernatore: Postea vero Ecclesiæ Algarbiensis Episcopo, et ejusdem Regni Armorum Gubernatore. It is a performance calculated to free the votaries of Rome not only from the obligations of civil but of *divine* authority; furnishing such distinctions,

LETTER VII.

that the magistrate should not expect, much less exact, obedience or submission in matters purely religious; and that, in things pertaining to conscience, it is the duty of the subject to act upon the principle of the apostles and primitive Christians; that is, to " obey God rather than men *." But then there is nothing in this sentiment, in the smallest degree, inconsistent with *civil obedience:* " rendering unto God the " things which are God's," is no objection to " rendering unto Cæsar the things " which are Cæsar's †." The Dissenters are so far from setting up the supposed interests of religion, or, as you express it, " spiritual men," or " spiritual causes," against lawful magistracy, or the peace

stinctions, evasions, and decisions, with regard to the most FLAGITIOUS and even UNNATURAL crimes, as amply instruct men how to commit them, *salvâ conscientiâ.* Is not this astonishing, in modern times, in a man of letters, and, as I have been informed, polite and conversible?

Tantum R*ELLIGIO* potuit suadere malorum!

* Acts v. 29. † Matth. xxii. 21.

and

and good order of society, that they allow of the exemption of none from the authority of the civil magistrate; holding all to be equally under his jurisdiction; and that no plea of sacred character, or of religion and conscience, is to be admitted in bar to his procedure, in matters of a criminal, or merely civil nature. And as, in their opinion, it is his duty to *protect* all *good subjects* in the profession of their religious principles; so, without any regard to their religious principles or professions, he is to *punish* all *offenders* against the *peace* of society. Now, how is this " setting up an " independent supremacy of their own, " where spiritual men and spiritual causes " are concerned?" If, as they say, all men are to judge for themselves, and act accordingly, in matters of faith and worship, and the salvation of their souls; if, in these respects, they are not to controul, usurp upon, and domineer over one another, and are at the same time to be *all alike subject to the civil magistrate*; this appears

pears to me to be so far from setting up an *imperium in imperio,* that it leaves no *imperium,* no supremacy, indeed, *no power at all,* in society, *but that* of the civil magistrate. These principles, therefore, can never issue in a distinct independent supremacy of those who profess them, whether *spiritual men* or others. The principles of the Papists, indeed, directly lead to and support this supremacy: the principles of the Dissenters are diametrically opposed to it.

And as their principles are quite of another nature, another genius and complexion, than those of the Papists; so are they, than those of the enthusiasts whom you have mentioned. I know no Dissenter on earth, who holds, that *dominion is founded in grace,* and that *the saints must rule the world;* or any principles which have the least tendency and aspect towards such a conclusion. On the contrary, they all to a man assert, that religion is so far from vesting in its professors a title to *dominion,*

minion, that it is no exemption from *civil subjection*. It is in matters of confcience only, they apprehend, they are alone accountable to God; and that not fo as to excufe thereby any criminal overt acts, inconfiftent with the peace of fociety: *thefe* the magiftrate muft punifh, from whatever principle they proceed, from any or none, and whatever plea of that fort is offered in their favour. Some enthufiafts formerly, particularly thofe you have cenfured, made one compofition of religion and politics; the Diffenters, on the contrary, keep them wholly diftinct, as being of a different nature, and relating to different purpofes, and different interefts; the one to the foul, the other to the body; the one to the prefent world, the other to the future. Thefe enthufiafts were ftrenuous affertors of the monarchy of King Jefus, that his kingdom was of this world: the Diffenters zealoufly maintain, in conformity with reafon and fcripture, that

" Chrift's

"Chrift's kingdom is not of this world*," and doth not at all interfere with the office of the magiftrate; who, in their opinion, is fupreme over all perfons within his dominions, of whatever religion, of any or none. I will venture to affirm, that it is impoffible to erect the fyftem of thefe enthufiafts, as a fuperftructure, on the principles of the Diffenters, as a foundation. The principles of the latter are totally incompatible with the whole fcheme of the former, and, of all others, moft effectually overturn and deftroy it. In a word, their principles with refpect both to church-authority and to civil government, are precifely the fame which the late Bifhop Hoadly advanced, and fupported in an unanfwerable manner, doing thereby fuch fervice to the caufe of true Proteftantifm, and of the royal fucceffion in the houfe of Hanover, as will always be remembered with gratitude by the true

* John xviii. 36.

friends of that august family, and of the liberties of their country.

I shall only add, in justice to Dr. Priestley, whom you call a willing critic, (I suppose, you mean one inclined to put not the most favourable construction upon your expressions,) that, I believe, every Dissenter, I am sure, every one with whom I have conversed, who had read that page in your Commentaries, which contains a comparison between the principles and the conduct of the Papists and the sectaries, understood you, in the most obnoxious passage of all, in the same sense in which he did; namely, as referring to the modern Dissenters; and were perhaps as much offended with it as he was: I refer to that clause, wherein you say, " As to " the Papists, their tenets are undoubted- " ly calculated for the introduction of all " slavery, both civil and religious; but it " may with justice be questioned, whether " the spirit, the doctrines, and the prac- " tice

"tice of the sectaries ARE better calcula-
"ted to make men good subjects *."

I shall not scruple to affirm, that there are no better subjects, and no better friends to the constitution of their country as a limited monarchy, defined and improved by the glorious Revolution, than the Protestant Dissenters †: they pray for the con-

---

* Comment. vol. iv. p. 52.

† "The Dissenters are sincere well-wishers to the civil "part of our present happy establishment; and they are to "be esteemed and loved for it," saith the late Abp. Secker, in his Letter to Mr. Walpole concerning bishops in America, p. 24, 25. Dr. Burton, the Archbishop's panegyrist (in his Commentariolus Thomæ Secker, &c. p. 27.) hath given a different character of certain persons, whom he stiles, "Dissentientium greges quidam:" After mentioning the Archbishop's scheme of sending bishops to America, he adds: fremunt tamen illico et tumultuantur *Dissentientium greges quidam* irritabiles et pervicaces; iidem in Republicâ Cives seditiosi, in Ecclesiâ Principatum adepti, Tyranni intolerabiles. Whether the author levels this invective against the Presbyterians and Independents in the colonies, or the Dissenters at home, I will not be positive. If he means the Americans, they perhaps would tell him, that he hath grosly misrepresented both their civil and their religious principles, and would excuse him on the score only of that noble privilege, which Atticus allows all rhe-
toricians,

continuance of the Proteſtant ſucceſſion in the preſent illuſtrious royal family, and for the *ſalus regis et populi*, in the words, and with the fervour, with which father

toricians: Conceſſum eſt Rhetoribus ementiri in hiſtoriis, ut aliquid dicere poſſint argutius. Cicero de claris oratoribus, c. 11. But if he means the Diſſenters, I am content to aſcribe it ſolely to his total ignorance of their character, otherwiſe he would know, that eccleſiaſtical authority, and much more eccleſiaſtical tyranny, in the hands of either preſbyters or biſhops, is their entire averſion. As for ſedition, that charge, 'I think, is unjuſt even againſt their anceſtors the puritans; who, in general, were not a whit more ſeditious, or more enemies to limited monarchy and lawful authority, than thoſe great patriots of the church of England, who at that time oppoſed the deſigns of an arbitrary court, and the dangerous incroachments of prerogative upon civil liberty. And as to their deſcendants the modern Diſſenters, let his oracle the Archbiſhop be their compurgator; who had reaſon to know them better than his panegyriſt, as he was not only born of diſſenting parents, but received his education, together with the late excellent Biſhop Butler, in one of their academies, under a tutor, whoſe great learning and abilities would have been no little honour to either of our univerſities: Circumſtances, by the way, which this gentleman, in his great ingenuity and liberality of ſentiment, hath thought proper to paſs over in ſilence; whether, becauſe he imagined, they would be a diſgrace to the Archbiſhop, or an honour to the Diſſenters, or both, I pretend not to determine.

Paul

LETTER VII.

Paul prayed for the republick of Venice in his dying moments: ESTO PERPETUA!

But I have done: you have promised to correct those passages in your next edition; and I have no doubt, you will make that correction in such a manner as will be entirely satisfactory.

In thus addressing you, Sir, I would not be thought to entertain a fondness for controversy. I know full well, how seldom it is, that controversies answer any valuable end. They often sour and imbitter mens minds, and give a keenness and acrimony to their tempers; besides engrossing a great deal of time and attention, which most men may employ to much better purposes. I am so convinced of this, that nothing should have engaged me to appear in the character of a polemical writer, even so far as I have now done, in laying before you, and the publick, the preceding remarks, if I had not been fully persuaded, that some positions and sentiments which you have advanced,

have

have an unfavourable aspect (and the more so as coming from an author of your distinguished reputation) on the glorious cause of religious liberty: a cause nearly connected with, and of great importance to, the interests of truth, and the present and future happiness of mankind.

Thus, Sir, have I freely, and I hope, inoffensively, pointed out some of the *supposed* blemishes in your otherwise excellent and elaborate work; which many, who have a great opinion both of the author and of his performance, wish to see corrected. And, I am persuaded, they will be so, as far as you shall be convinced they are *real* blemishes: Whether they are or not, must be left, Sir, to your consideration, and to the judgment of the impartial publick.

I am,

With great respect, &c.

Philip Furneaux.